To Pete,

Beat Navy!

~ Amerle

AMERICA'S
FAVORITE MASCOT

A HISTORY OF THE
Army Mule *at the* United States Military Academy

AMANDA VAN ESSEN WIRTH

Library of Congress Control Number: 2021937231

ISBN (paperback): 9781662910678
eISBN: 9781662910685

Wherever man has left his footprints in the long assent from barbarism to civilization, we find the foot print of a horse beside it.

-JOHN TROTWOOD MOORE

DEDICATION
AND ACKNOWLEDGMENTS

This book is dedicated to the men and women of the United States Armed Forces and all of the animals that have served with Americans side by side. Mules are often overlooked and lumped in with the horses, but have provided enormous support to the American military over the history of America.

This book would not be possible without the generous information and photos provided by various individuals.

The photos and stories in this book are provided by the personal collections of Willis Tomsen '54, Michael Lapolla '65, Walter Price '50, Steve Townes '75, Harrison Mann '12, David Nunneley, West Point Public Affairs Office, open-source online sites, U.S. Government fair use, and public domain. Special thanks to all who helped and who love our mules!

This book would also not be possible without the assistance of my husband and support of my kids. Thank you: Chris, Noah, and Tilly! I love you!

TABLE OF CONTENTS

CHAPTER ONE

Introduction

The Corps of Cadets at the United States Military Academy are not just some of the finest athletes in college sports, they are the next generation of world leaders, titans of industry, and defenders of freedom.

Since 1899, the Black Knight athletes have been shadowed (and at times overshadowed) by another long gray line—their mule counterparts. The mules have officially been the mascot at sporting events and public appearances since 1936. While the Bald Eagle has been America's national bird, symbol, and mascot since the founding of America, there's a favorite mascot: the Army mule.

Thanks to an endowment from Steve Townes, a 1975 graduate of West Point and former rabble rouser, the Army mule will be a fixture at West Point always.

The rabble rouser mule riders of current and past generations have created a sort of fraternity bound by the incredible opportunity each of them has had over the years to care for America's mascot.

It's impossible to capture all of the stories of the mules or describe the important role they played in the lives of some cadets. This book chronicles the background of the long gray line of America's mascot and some of the stories of those who have cared for them, as well as the history available for each of the mules in their long gray line.

All equines were banned from West Point after World War II; but with the help of SFC Robert P. Johnson, the mules were excluded from the ban and have represented the United States Military Academy faithfully ever since.

"Look back at man's struggle for freedom.

Trace our present day's strength to its source,

And you'll find that man's pathway to glory is strewn with the bones of
the horse.

-Unknown

Painted at Morgan Farm at West Point

How This Book Was Imagined and Created

This book is a collaboration of many mule fans and people committed to bettering the lives of American heroes. For decades mule riders have enjoyed the mules. The mules have been partners to the mule riders. The mules have been confidants. The mules most notably have been accomplices in shenanigans of epic proportions in tales not recounted until now.

Raider and Ranger II were retired to author Amanda Van Essen Wirth's family home in Grandville, Michigan in 2011. Steve Townes, the creator of the endowment for the West Point mules, contacted Amanda, introducing himself and sharing mule stories. At that point, Mr. Townes introduced Amanda to other mule riders. The mule riders shared their stories and adventures that surrounded the mules and their time at West Point.

The mule riders have created a sort of fraternity, and several of them stay in touch. They helped to introduce the author to other mule riders and people interested in the Army mule.

Hanniba I(L) Trotter (C) Pancho(R)
1960 Michie Stadium
Phil Florence'62 (L)
Ron Hines'61 (C-Top)
Rod Grannemann'61 (C-under)
Bill Robbins'63 (R)

What This Author Learned About Mules

When Raider and Ranger II came to live with me, I didn't know much about mules. I had grown up on a horse farm and had naturally assumed that mules were going to be pretty similar. Boy was I wrong! Mules are the pushiest animals imaginable. Stubborn as a mule is a phrase that is certainly fitting. They'll use their heads as weapons, and unlike horses, they know they're larger than humans and won't be pushed around. It's often said among horse people that you "urge a stallion, tell a gelding, but you ask a mare." Although most mules are males they are much more like mares and they must be asked.

When I've witnessed these mules interact with people, it's been amazing. They know exactly who they can take advantage of and exactly who doesn't like them. The funny thing is that they are putty in the hands of small children. I've seen countless little boys and little girls feed grass to Raider at parades and community events. He'll push around adults or anyone in authority, but I've never seen anything so gentle as Raider interacting with little kids.

The mules are hearty and tough, as we know, but I never imagined how much they would improve the shape of my pastures. The mules are weed eaters. They just plow right through thistles and burr bushes. It's been amazing to see them mow right through the weeds and clear the pasture.

Riding mules is the equine version of riding an ATV. Riding horses limits where one can go. They need more navigable trails than a mule. A mule can climb up rocks and mountainsides like a billy goat (but obviously better, since midshipmen are goats). Riding mules around the West Point wilderness and the Hudson River is an experience like none other.

The Long Gray Line of Army Mules

Mr. Jackson

Pancho "Skippy"

K.C. Mo

Hannibal

Trotter

Hannibal II

Buckshot

Spartacus

Ranger I

Black Jack

Traveller "Dan"

Trooper "Ernie"

Raider

Ranger II "George"

General Scotty

Ranger III

Stryker

Paladin

1899: Big Whitey

1936-1939: Mr. Jackson

1939-1948: Mr. Jackson and Pancho "Skippy"

1948-1957: Pancho and Hannibal

1957-1958 Hannibal, K.C. Mo, Trotter , Pancho

1958-1964: Hannibal, K.C. Mo. Trotter

1964-1969: K.C. Mo, Trotter, Hannibal II, Buckshot

1969-1972: Trotter, Hannibal II, Buckshot

1972-1973: Hannibal II, Buckshot

1973-1978: Hannibal II, Buckshot, Spartacus

1978-1980: Hannibal II, Buckshot, Spartacus, Ranger, Black Jack
    This seems to be the only time West Point had 5 mules.

1980-1986: Buckshot, Spartacus, Ranger, Black Jack

1986-1989: Spartacus, Black Jack, Ranger

1989-1994: Spartacus, Ranger

1994-1995: Spartacus, Traveller "Dan," and Trooper "Ernie" 1995-
        2002: Traveller, Trooper, Raider

2002-2011: Raider, General Scotty, Ranger II "George"

2011-2016: Stryker and Ranger III

2016-Present: Paladin, Stryker, and Ranger III

Over the years, many of the mules have worn saddle blankets custom made with the Army "A" and their names on them. This helps their fans get to know them better.

A family portrait .....

TOGETHERNESS -- They may not understand football, but these three Army mule mascots enjoy standing on the sidelines in Michie Stadium on autumn Saturdays. This week will be their final home opportunity of the season as Army hosts Bucknell. Ridden by cadets, the animals are well-trained and don't even shy from the cannon-fire that erupts when Army scores.

(Photo by Brennan)

This photo of a newspaper article was taken at the Mule Museum at the United States Military Academy. By looking at the date, one can figure out which mules were in the photo. It was the end of 1995. The mules were Raider, Traveller, and Trooper. This was one of Raider's first games, as he came to West Point in September 1995. Traveller and Trooper came to West Point in 1994. Spartacus retired earlier in the season.

Traveller and Trooper would retire seven years later, in 2002. Raider would stay at West Point for sixteen years.

The average time a mule serves at West Point is fifteen years.

Most mules serve in some capacity much longer than fifteen years, as many serve in the Army as pack mules or continue after their time at West Point to help soldiers with PTSD (post-traumatic stress syndrome).

Raider spoiled in his retirement by this auther and getting kisses from his "swisster," Greater Swiss Mountain Dog, Reese.

West Point History and Fun Facts from "A Brief History of West Point"

"West Point's role in our nation's history dates back to the Revolutionary War, when both sides realized the strategic importance of the commanding plateau on the west bank of the Hudson River. General George Washington considered West Point to be the most important strategic position in America. Washington personally selected Thaddeus Kosciuszko, one of the heroes of Saratoga, to design the fortifications for West Point in 1778, and Washington transferred his headquarters to West Point in 1779. Continental Soldiers built forts, batteries, and redoubts and extended a 150-ton iron chain across the Hudson to control river traffic. Fortress West Point was never captured by the British, despite Benedict Arnold's treason. West Point is the oldest continuously occupied military post in America.

Several Soldiers and legislators—including Washington, Knox, Hamilton, and John Adams—desiring to eliminate America's wartime reliance on foreign engineers and artillerists, urged the creation of an institution devoted to the arts and sciences of warfare.

President Thomas Jefferson signed legislation establishing the United States Military Academy in 1802. He took this action after ensuring that those attending the Academy would be representative of a democratic society.

Colonel Sylvanus Thayer, the "Father of the Military Academy," served as Superintendent from 1817 to 1833. He upgraded academic standards, instilled military discipline, and emphasized honorable conduct. Aware of our young nation's need for engineers, Thayer made civil engineering the foundation of the curriculum. For the final first half-century, USMA graduates were largely responsible for the construction of the bulk of the nation's initial railway lines, bridges, harbors, and roads.

After gaining experience and national recognition during the Mexican and Indian wars, West Point graduates dominated the highest ranks on both sides during the Civil War. Academy graduates, headed by generals such as Grant, Lee, Sherman, and Jackson, set high standards of military leadership for both the North and South.

Of 60 battles fought in the Civil War, 55 saw West Point graduates commanding on BOTH sides of the conflict. In the remaining battles, a West Point graduate commanded one of the two sides.

West Point has only around 4,000 cadets (total) because Congress mandates the number of cadets at the institution. Prior to 1964, the number was 2,529.

In World War I, Academy graduates again distinguished themselves on the battlefield. After the war, Superintendent Douglas MacArthur sought to diversify the academic curriculum. In recognition of the intense physical demands of modern warfare, MacArthur pushed for major changes in the physical fitness and intramural athletic programs. "Every cadet an athlete" became an important goal. Additionally, the cadet management of the Honor System—long an unofficial tradition—was formalized with the creation of the Cadet Honor Committee.

In 1964, President Johnson signed legislation increasing the strength of the Corps of Cadets 2,529 to 4,417 to keep up with the growth of the Corps, a major expansion of facilities began shortly thereafter.

Another significant development at West Point came when enrollment was opened to women in 1976. Sixty-two women graduated in the class of 1980. Today, 17% of all cadets are women—the same percentage as in the U.S. Army."[1]

It is rumored that the Highland Falls, New York McDonald's is actually located on West Point land and is the only McDonald's that delivers (at least before the invention of Uber Eats and the like).

Both General George Armstrong Custer and General George S. Patton graduated last in their respective classes, making them the class "goats." General Patton took five years to graduate from West Point even though it is mandatory that cadets graduate in four years.

Each graduate of West Point receives a Bachelor of Science degree. Upon graduation, a limited number of cadets are permitted to immediately attend graduate school. Army War College is where Senior leaders attend to advance their military careers.

The cover of the West Point Discovery Children's Book, 1996.

CHAPTER TWO

The Army Mules

Stryker and Ranger III leave their North Caroline home with no idea how their lives are going to change forever.

What is a Mule?

This description comes straight from the U.S. Army Field Manual 3-05.213 Special Forces Use of Pack Animals. "Mules are the hybrid product of a male donkey and a female horse. Male mules are called johns and female mules are called mollies or mare mules. Mollies are a cross between male donkeys and Belgium horse mares. Mollies generally have a gentler disposition than johns. Intelligence, agility, and stamina are all characteristics of mules. These qualities make mules excellent pack animals. Unlike horses, which carry about 65 percent of their weight on their front legs, mules carry 55 percent on their front legs. This trait makes them very well balanced and surefooted in rugged terrain."[2]

"Some people think stubbornness is a mule characteristic—stubborn as a mule! Mules are intelligent and possess a strong sense of self-preservation. A packer cannot make a mule do something if the mule thinks it will get hurt, no matter how much persuasion is used. Therefore, many people confuse this trait with stubbornness. Mules form close bonds with horses, especially mares. The bond is so close that mules willingly follow a mare. That is why a mare will usually be wearing a bell leading a string of mules. A wrangler, or mule skinner, can usually control an entire pack string simply by controlling the bell mare. At night in the back country, mule skinners can picket the bell mare and turn the mules loose. The mules will disperse and graze freely, yet remain close to the mare. Environmental impacts are reduced and the mules are easy to gather in the morning."[3]

"Young mules are naturally and easily startled, but if treated with great patience and kindness, can easily be broken in. All harsh treatment of any kind must be avoided or could prove to be fatal to successful training."[4]

Based on this author's observation of mules and conversations with mule experts, the following have been confirmed:

- Mules can be used in nearly every activity that horses can be used in. They can be ridden, pull carts, work cows, perform dressage, and anything in between. Although some horse shows will not allow mules and donkeys to participate for fear that they will frighten the horses, some experts have told me that donkeys and mules and zebras smell different to horses than horses do, and it can be frightening to horses not exposed to them previously.

- Donkeys have 62 chromosomes and horses have 64 chromosomes. Mules have 63 chromosomes, a result of their being a hybrid between a horse and a donkey. They are sterile. It is incredibly rare for a mule to reproduce. (More on that to come!)

- Mules make the most ridiculous noise, sounding like a combination of a horse whinny and a donkey bray. Each mule I have heard sounds different.

- Because of their unique breeding and hybrid nature, mules can come in nearly any shape and size. Some mules are miniature, at just three feet high. Some mules can be taller than six feet! Since donkeys can be different and horses are so diverse, the possibility of the offspring is nearly endless. Some zules and zonkeys have even been bred by crossing a donkey and a zebra!

- Mules can be any color except a true-horse pinto.

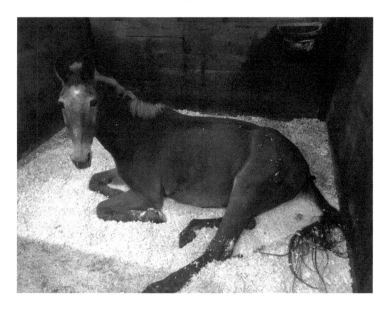

Raider enjoying afternoon nap

- Hinnies are more rare than mules. Hinnies come from a donkey mother and a horse father. It's rarely possible to tell a mule from a hinnie, but the hinnies are more rare. Since the mother is a donkey, hinnies are typically smaller than a mule; but obviously mules are already a broad range of shapes and sizes. Both hinnies and mules can be used in exactly the same disciplines as horses—under saddle, driving, dressage, or even cow events. Because of their hybrid nature, both the hinnies and the mules are more surefooted, can carry more, and require less care than a horse. They have more stamina as well.
- "Hinny" is also a term of endearment in England. "Hinny" is frequently used in place of where an American would use "honey."
- Mules are incredible jumpers and have been known to jump obstacles 150% of their height! In Southern states, mules are used to coon hunt. Raccoon hunting is similar to fox hunting—but instead of a fox, a raccoon is chased; and instead of a horse, a mule is used!
- Mules can be known for both their stubborn and their playful personalities.

Raider is a more playful mule and undoubtedly enjoyed his life as a mascot.

Mules in Warfare

Where there have been American Soldiers, there have been mules. Because of their easy keeping, their strength, and their durability, mules are ideal partners that have long carried what soldiers couldn't, to places that vehicles couldn't either.

Mules have carried heavy artillery through tough terrain and still carry heavy loads for Americans through the tough mountain terrains in places like Afghanistan.

In World War II, it became necessary to delivery mules to allies. One idea was to teach the mules to parachute in. Twelve mules were selected and placed into two groups of six. The first group was loaded onto a plane in what would be disastrous for the mules. The next six mules seemed to have known what happened and refused to be loaded onto the airplane.[5, 5b]

Mules in Modern Warfare

Today, mules are still used by both the Americans and the Taliban. The terrain in Afghanistan is mountainous and hard. Vehicles cannot travel successfully. Because of the altitudes and the rocket-propelled grenades, helicopters are sometimes unable to reach locations where soldiers are. If helicopters can't make it and ground vehicles can't make it, that leaves mules! Pack mules are at times critical for moving supplies in Afghanistan. So much so that there is an Army field manual for pack animals; and at the Marine Corps Mountain Warfare Training Center, marines and other troops are not just trained in land navigation and rifle marksmanship but also trained in how to manage a pack animal. They learn everything from packing the animal to caring for the animal, and basic veterinary care.[6]

CHAPTER THREE

The West Point Mules

Why a Mule?

Legend has it that in 1899, the Navy showed up with their goat to the Army–Navy game. Not to be out done, cadets brought a mule. The acquisition of the mule is a mystery. Some believe that the mule was purchased from a local ice deliveryman. Some believe that the mule was stolen. Personally, I think the mule was probably stolen. Several old West Point grads call the first mule Old Whitey.

West Point Mules and Celebrities

Perhaps the most underrated mascot in college football and essentially all sports, the West Point mule has spent decades entertaining the most influential people in the world.

The West Point mules have met athletes like Babe Ruth, celebrities such as Miss USA and Miss America, every American president, other world leaders, and of course, the long gray line of West Point graduates who have gone on to change the world.

Uga, the University of Georgia Bulldog; Buffy, the University of Colorado Buffalo; and Zeke the Wonder dog at Michigan State University are cherished parts of their respective university's heritage. None of those mascots have the history and stories the West Point mules have.

Below is Babe Ruth with two West Point cadets and one of the Army mules.

Pictured above is Miss USA 2010, Rima Fakih of Michigan, along with Harrison Mann (USMA 2012) and mules Ranger II and Raider.

The Long Gray Line Movie

"Maureen O'Hara starred in The Long Gray Line. Mule rider Bob Hinrichs, Class of 1955, is pictured left with Ms. O'Hara. Above is Ms. O'Hara with Hannibal. The Long Gray Line is a 1955 American drama film directed by John Ford on the life of Marty Maher. The story follows Maher's arrival at West Point and his progress from servant to beloved leader and teacher. The film also covers Maher's personal life, his romance and marriage to Mary O'Doonnell, played by Ms. O'Hara, and his declining years after her death. Willis "Tiny" Tomsen (class of 1954) was an extra in the film. Also in the film was Al Worden (class of 1955) who flew to the moon on Apollo 15."[7]

Mr. Jackson (1936-1948)

Mule biographies believed to have originated from goarmywestpoint.com and have been retold by generations of alumni. Not much is known about the official Army mules before 1936. Although the Army has used the mule as its mascot since 1899, and has from time to time had live mules on the grounds, the mules were not regulars at West Point until 1936.

"In 1936, Mr. Jackson became the first of the Academy's officially designated mascots. He arrived from the Remount Station at Fort Royal, Virginia. His military career started as pack mule with the Regular Army. He served for many years at West Point as the oldest mule in the Army.

Although joined by a second mascot in 1939, Mr. Jackson reigned as head mascot of the Army team until 1948. The football teams that he served won two national championships while compiling a record of 83 wins, 28 losses, and 9 ties.

Retired after the 1948 season, Mr. Jackson is said to have raised loud and vigorous objections when, in later years, younger mules were led from their stalls to participate in game activities. He remained at West Point until his death on January 4, 1961, at the ripe-old-age of 35 years."[8]

Mr Jackson (L) Pancho (R)
1948 Penn FB Game
Bob Makinney '49
Jim McDaniel '49
Charles Spettel '49

While countless stories online and the official West Point website state that Mr. Jackson was named for General Thomas "Stonewall" Jackson, as well as stories from cadets and graduates from West Point, some have doubts.

Many find it strange that West Point would name any mule especially their first mule after a confederate general. Perhaps by calling him Mr. Jackson instead of General Jackson and refusing to acknowledge his rank or his army as legitimate, it's a dig at General Jackson. General Jackson's death was an important event leading to the ultimate success of the North and he was a very skilled officer responsible for much of the confederate's success. He graduated high in his class from West Point which undoubtedly shaped his skills as an officer.

If Mr. Jackson was not named for General Jackson, he is perhaps simply named because he is half jackass. In a comic book from 1943 featuring the Army–Navy game, Mr. Jackson is introduced. The plot of the comic book sort of combines several years of unconfirmed mule stories and legends.

The comic starts out with Navy winning the game because they introduced a mascot: Bill the goat. In response to Bill the goat, Army cadets determine the goat is too lucky and they purchase a mule from an ice delivery man. They immediately take him to the tailor to have his Army blanket sewn. They decide to name him Jack, since he's half jackass. The Navy goat is walked over to meet Jack and Jack kicks him clear into the stands. Army won the game.

Mr. Jackson is buried somewhere at West Point in an unmarked grave.

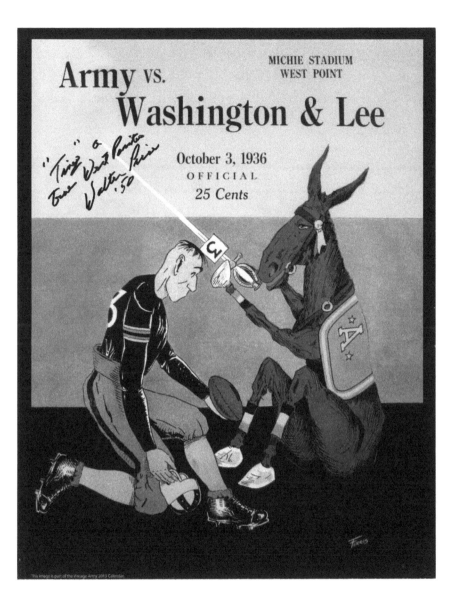

1926 football program featuring Mr. Jackson-the first Army football program depicting an Army mule.

Pancho "Skippy" (1939-1958)

"The second mascot, Pancho (sometimes called "Skippy"), was a small Ecuadorian burro. She was presented to the Military Academy in 1939 by her donor, Ambassador Colon Alfaro of Ecuador, the same year his sons Elroy and Jamie graduated from the Academy as foreign students.

At the 1942 Army–Navy game, Pancho appeared on the field disguised in a goat's skin and horns. Her rider, dressed in a midshipman's uniform, created quite a scene by riding what appeared to be the Navy goat into the Philadelphia Stadium.

These photos of Pancho with Hannibal show just how tiny Pancho was!

Pancho was a burro and not a mule, and one of only two females to serve. Technically, after World War II, only mules were allowed at West Point. Pancho, the burro must have blended in well!

Pancho retired in 1958, but stayed at West Point until 1962. Her final days were spent at a farm in Otisville, New York."[9]

Hannibal I (1948-1964)

"A third mule, Hannibal I, arrived in June 1948, after six years in the Regular Army. Hannibal I stood over fourteen hands high (a hand is four inches) and weighed nearly 1,000 pounds."

"He died on March 14, 1964, two days after being kicked by another mule."[10]

At the time of Hannibal I's death, there were two other mules on mascot duty at West Point—K.C. MO and Trotter. Both arrived in 1957.

According to Tiny Tomsen, Hannibal was born in 1942 and used as a pack mule in the Army. When he became a West Point Mascot, he was broke to ride by Walter Price of the class of 1950.

Hannibal was the longest tenured Mascot at West Point and is rumored to be the most intelligent.

While each mule is loved by its cadet handlers and many of the other cadets, it seems as though Hannibal was possibly the most beloved by the entire class.

Trotter, K.C. Mo, and Hannibal are pictured with J. Fred Muggs, celebrity chimp popular in the 1950's before heading to Busch Gardens and retiring to Florida with his "girlfriend" Phoebe B. Beebe.

Pancho(Front) Hannibal (Back-L)
Mr Jackson (Back-R)
1948 Michie Stadium
Robert Makinney '49

Trotter (L) Hannibal (C) Pancho (R)
1958 The Plains, West Point
Bill Murry '55 (L)
Don Echelbarger '59 (C)
Bob Drennan '59 (on Hannibal)
Rod Granneman '61 (R)

Trotter (L) Hannibal (R)
1958 Notre Dame
Bill Murry '53 (Top)
Bob Drennan '59 (Below)
Don Echelbarger '59 (R)

TRICK RIDERS SPICE HALF-TIME SHOW—The two Army mules brought to the game are put through their paces during a half-time by Don Eckelbarger, Emlenton, Pa., right, and top to bottom, Bill Murry, Corpus Christi, Tex. and Bob Drennan, Polo, Ill., riding double-decker at left.
—Photo by Tribune Staff Photographer

33

K.C. MO (1957-1969)

"K.C. MO (pronounced "kay-see-moe") was sometimes hard to ride and occasionally threw his rider off completely. He was retired to pasture at Fort Meade, Maryland, on May 13, 1969."[11]

Trotter (1957-1972)

"Trotter was a famous mule even before he became an Army mascot. While assigned to the 35th Quartermaster Pack Company at Fort Carson, Colorado, he became the only mule known to have mastered four gaits—walk, pace, canter, and trot. Many mules are unable to hold a gait at all, but Trotter was able to keep a gait for eight hours—or about fifty miles. Trotter's assignment to West Point was made possible after his pack company deactivated in 1956 and he was sold to the Colorado Springs Rodeo Association. The Association, in turn, presented him to the Military Academy at the Army–Nebraska football game in September 1957. He was also retired to a farm in Otisville, New York, in 1972. Foaled in 1946. He stood 15 hands high and weighed 1200 pounds."[12]

The description of Trotter is found in the Mule Museum at West Point.

TROTTER

TROTTER WAS A FAMOUS MULE EVEN BEFORE HE BECAME AN ARMY MASCOT. WHILE ASSIGNED TO THE 35TH QUARTERMASTER PACK COMPANY AT FORT CARSON, CO, HE BECAME THE ONLY MULE KNOWN TO HAVE MASTERED FOUR GAITS- WALK, PACE, CANTER, AND TROT. MANY MULES ARE UNABLE TO HOLD A GAIT AT ALL, BUT TROTTER WAS ABLE TO KEEP A GAIT FOR EIGHT HOURS- OR ABOUT 50 MILES.

TROTTER'S ASSIGNMENT TO WEST POINT WAS MADE POSSIBLE AFTER HIS PACK COMPANY WAS DEACTIVATED IN 1956 AND HE WAS SOLD TO THE COLORADO SPRINGS RODEO ASSOCIATION. THE ASSOCIATION IN TURN PRESENTED HIM TO THE MILITARY ACADEMY AT THE ARMY-NEBRASKA FOOTBALL GAME ON SEPTEMBER 28, 1957. FOALED IN 1946, HE STOOD 15 HANDS HIGH AND WEIGHED 1200 POUNDS. HE WAS RETIRED TO OTISVILLE, NY IN 1972.

Trotter Goes to West Point

WESTERN HORSEMAN readers will be interested to know that Trotter, one of the famous Army mules featured in the article *Last of the Best* (March 1957), is now at West Point.

Trotter was presented to the U.S. Military Academy and the Corps of Cadets by the Pikes Peak or Bust Rodeo Association, Colorado Springs, Colo., at the half-time ceremonies of the Army-Nebraska football game in late September. Thayer Tutt, president of the rodeo association, was accompanied by a delegation of other Pikes (Continued on page 44)

• Trotter and "Murph" Bryant stand at attention for the ceremonies.

Photos by U.S. Signal Corps

• Members of the Pikes Peak or Bust Rodeo Association accompanied Trotter to West Point, and filed onto the gridiron in Michie Stadium for the presentation ceremonies.

• Cadet Thomas H. Claffey (center), mascot rider, puts the Army blanket on Trotter as Coloradoans "Murph" Bryant and Charles Casey witness the transfer.

• Thayer Tutt, president of the Pikes Peak or Bust Rodeo Association, makes the presentation. First Captain and Brigade Commander, Cadet Robert F. Durkin accepts the mule as Miss Margaret Schweiker, Queen of Queens, from the University of Nebraska, and Cadet Thomas Claffey look on.

JANUARY, 1958

• Trotter was the center of attention at the half-time in Michie Stadium as mascot rider Cadet Thomas Claffey rode the famed mule around the football field before the crowd who had come to see the Army-Nebraska game. Trotter prances with pride as one who came "up through the ranks" to West Point.

Trotter as a Pack mule on his way to the United States Military Academy.

Trotter received a proper sendoff from his old Army pals.

Hannibal II (1964-1980) and Buckshot (1964-1986)

"The Corps of Cadets officially accepted Hannibal II and Buckshot during half-time of the Army–Pittsburgh game in November 1964. Sixteen years later, at another Army–Pittsburgh game, Hannibal II was officially retired due to bad health. He retired to Fort Huachuca, Arizona. Buckshot, a female, weighing about 1,000 pounds and standing just under 15 hands tall, was foaled in 1959. She came to West Point from Colorado Springs, Colorado, as a gift from the Air Force Academy in the fall of 1964. USMA cadets presented the Air Force with a ceremonial sword in return."

"Hannibal II (originally called Jack) served as an Army mascot from 1964 until 1980. Hannibal II got his name from the Hannibal, Missouri Chamber of Commerce, which presented him to the Military Academy on October. 13, 1964."

"Buckshot retired at the age of 27 to Elba, Alabama on July 10, 1986. Her retirement ceremony was a formal one, with then Superintendent Lt. Gen. Willard W. Scott, Jr. presiding. She was pastured on the farm of Lt. Col. (USAR) Kenneth D. Strong, a former mule rider."[13]

Hannibal II

Buckshot

Note the Air Force sweater and the Army "A." It's unlikely there are other photos of anyone from the Air Force Academy leading an Army mule.

Spartacus (1973-1994)

"Spartacus (also called "Frosty" because of his white muzzle) weighed about 1,200 pounds, stood 15 hands tall, and was foaled in 1969. The Missouri Farmers Association purchased him from the Missouri Draft Horse and Mule Breeders Association. Missouri Governor Warren E. Hearns presented Spartacus to the Corps of Cadets in the spring of 1973 in Jefferson City. His first public appearance as an Army Mule Mascot was at the Army–Notre Dame football game in November 1973."

"Spartacus retired to pasture at the age of 25 to the Collins, Mississippi farm of Mr. Ernest Napier, father of Ed Napier, a former mule rider. Lt. Gen. Howard D. Graves, then USMA superintendent, presided over a formal retirement ceremony during half-time at the Army–Temple football game on September 24, 1994."[14]

Ranger I (1978-1994)

"Ranger I was formally presented to the Corps of Cadets by the Ranger Association of World War II during pre-game ceremonies at the Army–Virginia football game in September 1978. Showing his pedigree as the son of a Percheron draft mare and a Spanish jack, Ranger I was a modestly large mule, standing at 15.2 hands. He was foaled in 1973."[15]

Although Ranger I was given to the Corps of Cadets by the Ranger Association of World War II, Ranger I became the start of a new mule tradition thanks to an endowment from Steve Townes.

A requirement of the endowment is that there is always a mule at West Point named Ranger in honor of the Army Rangers.

Spartacus (L)
Ranger (C)
Black Jack (R)
1989

Trophy Point

Traveller "Dan" (1990-2002)

"Traveller (also known as Dan) arrived at West Point, appropriately enough, on the same day that the USMA Class of 1994 started their West Point experience on July 2, 1990. Standing 16 hands and weighing 1,200 pounds, Traveller is one of the largest mules to have served as an Army Mule Mascot. He was named by the Mule Riders for his ability to do certain fancy steps, such as sidestepping. He was foaled in 1982."[16]

Black Jack (1978-1989)

"Black Jack was presented to the Corps of Cadets by then Senator Albert E. Gore, Jr. of Tennessee on October 25, 1985, as part of the First Annual Lynchburg Mule Show and Letting at Lynchburg, Tennessee. Foaled in 1978 in Gatlinburg, Tennessee, he weighed 1,000 pounds and stood nearly 15 hands. His Tennessee Walking Horse heritage was evident in his facial features and jet-black color. Black Jack died of cancer of the spleen on Dec. 7, 1989, just two days before the Army–Navy football game."[17]

Senator Gore is often given credit for procuring the mule for West Point. In fact, according to several graduates, Jack Daniels distillery actually purchased and donate the mule to West Point.

Although Black Jack only served for four years, he was popular among cadets.

Below is a photo of a newspaper clipping from the mule museum. Black Jack was modeling the process of the Army A for the local paper.

Cadet Leonard A. Kortekaas bleaches the first "A" on Black Jack's posterior for cameraman Pe Martini, while Cadet Mike Ryan tries to get the reluctant mule's attention. Black Jack simply snort "That's not my best side.

Below is a drawing of the beloved mule.

Trooper "Ernie" (1994-2002)

"Trooper (also known as Ernie) arrived on September 28, 1990. His love for donuts each morning was quickly adopted by the other mules. He stands 15 hands, weighs in at approximately 1,000 pounds, and was foaled in July 1981. Trooper is a highly trained saddle-type mule and has appeared and competed in many livestock shows and rodeos. Both Traveller and Trooper were retired during the Army-Holy Cross football game on September 7, 2002, to spend their retirement together on the Wye Mountain Branch of the Rasputin Mule Farm in Bigelow, Arkansas, owned by Judge William Wilson, Jr." (even though Judge William Wilson, Jr. was a Navy man).[18]

Traveller and Trooper were celebrated when they retired to their final home in Arkansas.

Army mules retire in rural Arkansas

On Sept. 9, 2002, the Wye Mountain Branch of the Rasputin Mule Farm in Bigelow, which is owned by U.S. District Judge William "Bill" Wilson, Jr., and served by First Electric, became the new home for Traveller and Trooper, faithful mascots for the United States Military Academy at West Point since 1990.

How did these proud symbols of the long gray line retire to Arkansas from their assignment at West Point? The story starts with a call from Bob Lyford, senior vice president and general counsel for Arkansas Electric Cooperative Corp., to Wilson shortly after the December 2001 Army-Navy football game. Lyford, who had just completed five years of service as a presidential appointee on the Academy's Board of Visitors, had learned that the retirement of Trooper and Traveller was imminent. His call was to see if his friend, who had owned, traded, and raised mules for years, would be interested in two more.

"It took only seconds for Wilson to respond, 'You bet I am. What do I have to do to get them?'" Lyford said.

The next four months were spent supplying his bona fides as a mule aficionado to the veterinarian at West Point and waiting to see if he got selected. In April he got the call that the superintendent of the Academy, Lt. Gen. William J. Lennox, had approved of the retirement of the mules to Wilson's farm. Wilson's interest in taking both mules was critical to the decision, Lyford said.

"Some candidates only expressed interest in one mule," Lyford said. "The veterinarian believed that because the mules had become such close stable mates, separation would actually result in depression and other health problems for the two mules."

Wilson didn't hesitate at the chance to acquire the mules.

"When Bob Lyford told me about their impending retirement, I immediately thought it would be a great honor to provide a retirement for these Army mules," Wilson said. "Although I served in the Navy, I feel kindly toward retirees from all branches of our armed forces."

The actual retirement of Trooper and Traveller did not occur, however, until a "change of command ceremony" took place at halftime of the Army-Holy Cross game on Sept. 7, 2002, which was the season opener for the Army Black Knights at Michie Stadium on the Hudson River.

Traveller, who weighs 1,200 pounds and stands at 16 hands (a hand is 4 inches), is one of the largest mules to have served as an Army Mule Mascot. Also known as Dan prior to coming to West Point, Traveller is 20 years old.

Coincidentally, his name was suggested by an Arkansan who was the senior cadet mule rider when Dan arrived at the Academy. Trooper (also known as Ernie), loves donuts, stands 15 hands, weighs approximately 1,000 pounds and was foaled in 1981. He is a highly trained saddle-type mule and had appeared in many rodeos prior to his arrival at West Point.

Cobbs Believe It Or Not, 1996 World Champion Gaited Mule.

Army's, Troopers, a close friend, and his grandson, Kyle Robinson, enjoy an outing at the mule farm.

The halter on Traveller, presented by the City of Little Rock Oct. 19, is Army's gold color. Traveller got a black one. The brass plate has their name and date on it.

Bob Lofland teaches friends with one of the miniature donkeys.

Raider (1995-2011)

Raider is this author's favorite mule. Formerly known as "Joker," Raider was the senior mule. "He arrived September 23, 1995, and was formally welcomed to the Academy at a pre-game ceremony prior to the Army–Colgate football game on October 28, 1995. He was foaled in 1989 by a Missouri Fox Trotter Champion mare and sired by a Kibler's Jack. He is sorrel (red) in color with a star in the center of his forehead and an "R" tattooed on his left hip.

In October 1992 Raider was loaned to the USMA cadets by his owner, Jim Robertson of Wayland, Missouri, to serve as a "surrogate" mule mascot for the Army–Quincy University soccer game at Quincy, Illinois. Raider was donated to the Academy by the Quincy Notre Dame High School Foundation through the efforts of Herb Wellman."[19]

Raider was retired in December, 2011. His last official duty was the Army–Navy Football game in Washington, D.C. Raider was retired with Ranger II to this author's parents' farm, Bear Creek Farm in Grandville, MI where Tonja Van Essen and Amanda Wirth cared for them. Raider spent his first summer at his new home making public appearances at community events and walking in a Memorial and Fourth of July Parade. Raider has served as a therapy mule from time to time at Bear Creek Farm assisting wounded warriors with PTSD. Raider passed away in 2020. Just prior to his death, he was the only living retired mascot.

Raider and General Scott at an Army Navy football game.

Ranger II "George" and General Scott (2002-2011)

The two mules, accepted into the Corps of Cadets during the Army–Holy Cross football game on September 7, 2002, were donated by Steve Townes, a 1975 USMA graduate and former head rabble rouser. Ranger II (also known as George) is the second mule named Ranger. "He is named in honor of the 75th Ranger Regiment. He is black in color and was foaled on July 12, 1997. His mother was a quarter-horse mare and his father was a standard jack. He came to USMA from Independence, Kansas. Ranger II was a trail-riding mule prior to becoming an Army mule mascot."[20]

General Scott (also known as Scotty) is named for Lt. Gen. (Ret.) Willard W. Scott, Jr., former USMA Superintendent and avid Army mule supporter. His name was selected by Army fans from four suggested names (Thunder, General Scott, Warrior, and Storm) on the Army Sports website (www.goarmysports.com).

Both mules were retired with Raider in December, 2011 at West Point. Raider served one more time as the mascot at the 2011 Army–Navy football game on December 6, 2011 in Washington, D.C. During that weekend he was stabled at Arlington. Raider has seen more American history than a lot of Americans!

Ranger II and Raider had become so attached that they were retired to the same farm. Ranger II accompanied Raider to community events and parades, hosted farm tours, and on a couple of occasions was a part of political events.

Ranger II passed away over Veteran's Day weekend in 2013.

General Scotty was retired to Betty Williams. Betty says, "I fell in love with his big, kind eyes during my husband's deployment to Keller Hospital. We found out they were retiring him a year later on a return deployment and put together a packet. We weren't sure where he would end up, or how much patience and understanding he would be allotted with his 'independent thinking.' We were willing to take a chance with him and if he didn't make a safe mount, he could live out the rest of his days grazing in our pastures. Fortunately, he has taken well to the trail, and with less than 30 hours of arena work, has acclimated himself to motorized equipment. He just needed some consistency and treats :). He is such a sweety!" Sadly, General Scotty has also passed away.[21]

Community Features and Photos

Mascots keep heritage alive at events

Story and photos by Emily Tower

Three happy fellows named Scotty, George and Raider just might have the most pleasant job in the Army.

They have all of their meals brought to them, have a team of cadets and a specialist bathe them and comb their hair, and their official duties involve rolling in the dirt, lounging in the sun and munching away on special food.

Children spoil them. West Point alumns wait to pamper them when they retire from the Army.

But when a mission comes along, the trio dutifully don historic uniforms and meet the day's challenge.

West Point Families and cadets can meet Scotty, George and Raider at the first football game of the season today when the Black Knights take on Temple at Michie Stadium. They'll be the ones with long, fuzzy ears and large nostrils sniffing for carrots.

As Army's mascots, the three mules will be standing on the sidelines with their cadet riders — Firstie Micah Lockhart, Cows Keri Anderson and Jacob Haag and Yearling Oakland McCulloch — to remind football players and fans of their roots.

Long before Scotty, George and Raider wore the Army saddle, mules were used to haul cannons

Army mule mascot Ranger II, also known as George, enjoys one of his favorite treats -- a nibble of grass.

and equipment and to carry Soldiers, which is why the West Point mules wear replica historic cavalry saddles, bridles and breast straps while on duty.

A mule first represented the U.S. Military Academy in 1899 when an officer decided the football team needed a mascot at the Army-Navy game because Navy had a goat, Lockhart said.

So, a white mule was released from his ice wagon pulling duties and dressed in fine black, gold and gray for the game. The mule brought good luck, and Army won that meeting, 17-5.

Mules appeared at football games until all equines were banned from West Point after World War II. The work of Sgt. 1st Class Robert P. Johnson, however, began the mascot program at the academy when he was able to keep two mules and a donkey after the ban.

Since then, 15 mules have had official mascot duty — including one female, Buckshot, who was a gift in the mid-1960s from the Air Force Academy.

Raider is the eldest of the three current Army mules. He's 19 years old and the favorite of Spc. Carol Albino, the animal care specialist who tends to the mules. As the most experienced, Raider is calm and handles his job well, she said.

Scotty, on the other hand, "is scared of everything — strollers, sun movement, wind, his own hair when we clip it," Albino said.

Scotty's official name is General Scott. The 9-year-old mule was named after retired Lt. Gen. Willard Scott Jr., a former U.S. Military Academy superintendent. He might be the youngest, but he is by far the tallest of the three mules. His ears alone are a foot tall.

Haag thinks Scotty is so tall because one of Scotty's parents was a draft horse. Mules are a cross between a horse and a donkey.

George is a nickname for Ranger II, who was named in honor of the 75th Ranger Regiment, a light infantry unit that predates the Revolutionary War and is best known for landing on Omaha Beach during D-Day in World War II, which inspired the motto "Rangers lead the way."

George, 11, is shy, but proud and knows he often is admired as

The Army's official mule mascots — Ranger II, also known as George, left; General Scott; and Raider -- are ridden at football games by a team of four cadets. The cadets who ride the mules are Yearling Oakland McCullough, on George; Cow Jacob Haag, on General Scott; Firstie Micah Lockhart, standing; and Cow Keri Anderson, on Raider.

the best-looking mule, Lockhart said. He also has a sweet tooth and loves to eat peppermint candy, Anderson said.

When fans feed the mules, though, Albino requests they only bring fresh carrots or apples and let the cadet riders provide the more unusual treats.

West Point Families can visit the mules any time and can get the best view of them when the mules are in their paddock behind the Vet Clinic in Bldg. 630.

Visitors are not allowed inside the paddock, but they may pet the mules and feed them if the mules get close.

If visitors forget to bring carrots or apples, a handful of grass suits the mules just fine, Albino said. And just the rustle of a carrot bag or the scent of grass should entice the mules to come investigate. Just remember to offer the food on a flat palm so fingers aren't accidentally bitten, Albino said.

Visitors also may check out a small mule museum from 8 a.m.-noon and 1-4 p.m. weekdays, excluding federal holidays, most training holidays and the last day of each month, at the Vet Clinic.

The museum features history about the mule mascots, their supporters and equipment used to care for them.

Mule admirers also may visit Scotty, George and Raider at football games. They attend the Army-Navy game and all home games, where they are available for photographs and rides for children — mule mood permitting.

Knowing a few tips can make a mule visit more successful, Lockhart said. Being calm around the animals will help them stay calm. Bright colors and loud noises

General Scott, Ranger II, and Raider were favorites during their time at the United States Military Academy. Shown on this page is one of the articles written about them in the Pointer View at the start of the 2008 school year. The evening this paper was printed, Army kicked off their 119th season. Unfortunately, they lost 35–7 to Temple.

Raider and Ranger II walk out of Michie Stadium for the final time.

Ranger II and Raider stand at attention while they are released from duty in Michie Stadium, December, 2011.

Stryker and Ranger III Arrive

From Mike Strasser, West Point Public Affairs:

"West Point, N.Y. (December 13, 2011). Ranger III and Stryker made their public debut at West Point during a ceremony on December 8th at Michie Stadium. The two new Army Mule Mascots were welcomed by the Corps of Cadets and other guests, while Raider and Ranger II were officially retired from service. Their arrival was long-awaited, as they have spent nearly four years being conditioned for their new assignment at the U.S. Military Academy.

They've already been exposed to the military environment at Fort Bragg, N.C., where Maj. Anne Hessinger works as an Army veterinarian. She previously owned the two mules and has gotten them familiar with firecrackers, gun shots, tarps, balloons, umbrellas, flowers—any peculiar elements and environments they may come across during their tenure as Army Mule Mascots. They'll also be able to handle the occasional cannon fire when the football team scores touchdowns at Michie Stadium.

"As long as the riders stay quiet on them, the mules won't mind," Hessinger said. "They'll hear it the first time and be like, 'what's that?' and then the second time they'll ignore it. That's how adaptable they can be." She said Ranger II and Stryker will have no problem leading teams onto the field, carrying flags and interacting with fans.

"They can be more than just statues standing on the sidelines," she said.

In years past, some mascots were able to perform extended gaits and a few trick moves, but Hessinger said these new mules were conditioned to pulling wagons and hauling logs rather than showboating.

Ranger III and Stryker in their first official act as West Point mules.

"They're broke as a team, so there's potential, down the road, to getting a harness for them and buying a wagon and being able to drive them that way. They've worked as a pair and that's why they're so much alike."

They're also brothers, perhaps from the same father, Hessinger believes.

"It makes a difference that they're brothers in the fact that they've been together their whole lives so they feed off each other like the Army's battle buddy system," she said.

"They've always been each other's battle buddy and the more things they do together the better they'll be." Hessinger said if one appears more nervous than the other, the calmness of the one can reassure the other. "They can be that support system for each other," she said. "But it's funny because they also love to fight.

"They work hard and they play hard." Having trained them for so long, Hessinger said it is sad to see them go.

"It's hard for me because they're a part of my family now. They're my kids," she said. "Leaving them behind is a little hard, but I hope to get them back eventually." It will also give her a reason to visit West Point again.

Class of 2013 Cadet Nels Estvold and the other cadet mule riders enjoyed a 30-minute session with the new mules upon their arrival to West Point. Estvold described Ranger III and Stryker as steady and stable successors. "We were all pretty excited to finally have them here," Estvold said. "We basically been waiting an entire year for their arrival, so once the saddles were on, it was great to finally ride them."

At least two riders will work with Ranger III and Stryker every day, which means Estvold will have a chance to ride the new mules two or three times each week. The departure of their former colleagues was bittersweet as the cadets led them off the field.

Estvold was partial to Raider and partnered with him the most. But all mule riders eventually come to know each mule by their individual personalities and traits. "They've been around ever since we've been here, so in a way, they're part of our family here," Estvold said.

Steve Townes, a former Army officer with the 75th Ranger Regiment, was proud that Ranger III will carry on an Army tradition at West Point. "My only stipulation as the permanent mule donor in perpetuity is that one of the Army mules will always be named Ranger in honor of all Rangers, living and dead," Townes said. Townes, a Class of 1975 graduate and former West Point mule rider, met with the current group of cadet riders."

"I told them this is a 113-year tradition and is part of the permanent brand image of West Point," he said. "I told them to take good care of the mules and have fun."[22]

(Editor's Note: The third Army Mule Mascot, General Scott, was not in attendance at his retirement ceremony. Raider, although officially retired, made his last official appearance as an Army Mule Mascot at the Army–Navy football game on Dec. 10.)

BEAT NAVY!!

The Long Gray Mule Line

Hannibal
1953 Howze Field
George Perrin '54

Ranger II and Stryker with their mule riders at Michie Stadium.

Ranger III and Stryker (2011-Present)

Ranger III and Stryker are the first pair of brothers to arrive at West Point. They've been trained together and are the first pair of mules that can pull a cart or a wagon. As of the writing of this book, West Point and cadets have yet to take advantage of that.

I was fortunate to meet Ranger III and Stryker during graduation week in May 2012. I was expecting the naughtiness I witnessed with Ranger II and Raider. Stryker and Ranger III were so well behaved! They were very calm and had some quirks. Stryker doesn't like his ears touched, which is problematic when attempting to put a bridle on him. You have to undo the top part of it and put the bit in with one hand while the other attempts to hold the top of the bridle together and pull it up. It's quite the juggling trick that I couldn't master. Although they look nearly identical, Stryker has a forelock (the bushy hair between his eyes on his forehead) and Ranger III is clean shaven.

Ranger III and Stryker live at the historic Morgan Farms a little drive away. At first I was disappointed with this move as I thought that it was a disservice to the cadets. But the Morgan Farm is beyond what one can imagine. I will not do it justice describing it. Nestled in the mountains and forested acres of West Point, the farm is heaven to any horse enthusiast and history buff like myself. The custom U.S. bits, the brass West Point crests on bridles, and the saddles engraved with past equestrian events and historic feats are amazing.

Meeting one or two members of the Mule Long Grey Line is a privilege in itself. In my case, I was able to ride Stryker through picturesque West Point. The thing about well-behaved mules is they act like horses. They're well-behaved, not mule-y. They listen to leg cues and respond to the bit. Ranger III and Stryker both did that, but what was amazing was that they still rode like mules. Mules are plows.

Taking Stryker out through the forests at West Point is something I'll never forget. There are trees and wilderness that have seen hundreds of years of American history. There are old stone walls built by the first Americans.

There are training sites for today's warriors. The past, present, and future of West Point rolls together in what seems like untouched beautiful forestry.

Stryker brought me on an adventure I'll never forget and I'm grateful to him.

The Mule Change of Command 2011

A change of command ceremony is a military tradition that transfers responsibility of a command or unit from one leader to the next. The Following is an email from Steve Townes to Tiny Tomsen, Walter Price, Michael Lapolla, and Jim Kennedy.

"Gentlemen:

"We Won! Pass on the word! The donation ceremony and press photos with the Superintendent will be on Dec. 7th at 3pm on The Plain. This video refers to the Michie Stadium "induction" ceremony on Dec. 8th. It's turning into quite the big deal. They are doing some special press coverage, just prior to the Army-Navy Game. These mules were drawn from the equine training group at Ft. Bragg...think "Special Forces Mules." And I should note that Ranger "III" is HUGE.

"Please feel free to share with others! Especially the whole class of 1954!"[23]

The "Mule Committee," an informal group of former mule riders and enthusiasts, stays in touch and plots new adventures for the mules from time to time. This is an example of the enthusiastic email exchanges.

Paladin (2016-Present)

Paladin joined the half-brother duo, Stryker and Ranger III, in 2016. Paladin is a couple hands shorter than his pals primarily because his mother is a thoroughbred as opposed to a Percheron like the other two. Paladin is still serving at West Point.

Paladin at the 2018 Reunion Parade with Bob and Jeanne Sullivan

Black Jack Version 2

Today, the Army mules are often accompanied by their other furry friend, Black Jack. Black Jack is named in honor of former mule, Black Jack.

This Black Jack is not as exciting as the real live mules but is allowed in more places than his mule friends.

During the Army Navy football weekend, Black Jack made the rounds in Washington D.C. visiting his friends at the Department of Defense.

Pictured above is Black Jack with Secretary of Defense Leon Panetta at the Pentagon in 2012.

Above, Black Jack is pictured with Deputy Defense Secretary Bob Work in 2014.

CHAPTER FOUR

The West Point Mule Riders

Walter Price aboard Hannibal in 1949. Prior to West Point, Walter Price was in the cavalry unit at Oklahoma Military Academy

The first official mascot was in 1936. The following is a listing of mule riders and the class they graduated with. Nearly 50 mule riders over the years were willing to contribute stories or share memories of the mules from their time at West Point.

1938	Jack Kelsey	1945	Geoffrey Keyes	1952	Charles Harvey	1957	Thomas McCrary
1938	Frederick Wright Jr.	1945	Strathmore McMurdo	1952	Peter Withers	1957	George O'Grady
1939	Robert Hunter	1946	Frederick Alderson	1953	Burden Brentnall	1958	Thomas Claffey
1939	Wayne O'Hern	1946	John Bartholf	1953	Samuel Fisher Jr.	1958	Richard Thomas
1939	Stanley Scott	1946	Needham Mewborn	1953	Robert Martin	1959	Donald Eckelbarger
1940	John Dwyer	1947	Robert Koch	1954	Richard LeCroy	1959	William Murry
1940	Wallace Hackett	1947	Walter Lukens	1954	Jackson Munsey	1960	Robert Drennen
1940	William Saunders	1947	Edwin Robertson	1954	George Perrin	1960	Michael Field
1941	Robert Brinson Jr.	1948	Denman Long	1954	James Surber	1961	Rodney Granneman
1941	Robert Johnson	1948	George Thomas	1955	Joseph Davis	1961	Ron Hines
1941	Straughan Kelsey	1948	Samuel White	1955	Robert Hinrichs	1962	James Corr
1942	James Bartholomees	1949	Robert Makinney	1955	Lawrence Stockett	1962	Phil Florence
1942	Sevarino Martinez Jr.	1949	James McDaniel	1956	Paul Hayne	1963	Wendell Gideon
1943	John Baer	1949	Charles Spettel	1956	Al Hoffman	1963	Arthur Hall
1943	William Brice	1950	John Jennings	1956	Aaron Loggins	1963	William Robbins
1943	George Danforth Jr.	1950	Walter Price	1956	John Wall	1964	Michael Griffith
1943	Everard Meade Jr.	1950	Ralph Stevenson	1956	Sidney Weinstein	1964	Randy Kunkel
1944	Charles Johnson	1951	Patrick Brian	1957	Jack Adams	1965	James Hall
1944	George Wear	1951	Richard Guidroz	1957	Donald Bowman	1966	Eugene Atkinson

24

Mule Riders: Koch, Lukens, Robertson

Mr Jackson (L) Poncho (R)
1946 Goat-Engineer FB Game
Robert Koch '47 (L)
Walter Lukens '47 (Up)
Edwin Robertson (R)

MULERIDERS
Long, White, Thomas

Mr. Jackson (L) Poncho (R)
1947 Location?
Denman Long '48 (L)
Sam White '48 (Up)
George Thomas '48 (R)

1966	Robert Kesmodel	1975	David Bear Jr.	1988	Michael Ryan	1998	Brett Judkins
1967	Ray Heath	1975	Steve Townes	1989	Douglas Gels	1998	Thomas Laybourn
1967	Kenneth Strong	1975	William Troy	1989	Chelsea Ortiz	1999	Tessa Burns-Snodgrass
1968	Robert Beahm	1977	Robert Goodman	1989	Sheryl Tullis	1999	Cecil Nix
1968	David Gerard	1977	Jay Kitzrow	1990	Scott O'Hearen	2000	Karl Hanson
1968	Jim Llewellyn	1978	Darcy Anderson	1990	Beth Richards	2001	Andrew Hanson
1969	James Rowan	1978	Michael Silva	1991	Shannon Beebe	2001	Andrew Herzberg
1970	Dana Newcomb	1979	William Sandbrook	1991	Luke Knittig	2002	Bryan Hart
1970	Jak Smith	1980	Curtis Balcer	1992	Don Bice	2003	Gina Romaggi
1971	Ronald Munden	1983	Brent Bredehoft	1992	James Frick	2004	Brian Hatalla
1971	Lyle Nelson	1983	Richard Hall	1993	Jeffrey Blaney	2005	James Alfaro
1972	Michael Deegan	1983	Shawn Wiant	1993	Joseph Napier III	2007	Alfredo Volio
1972	Paul Eaton	1984	Kyle Haase	1994	Karsten Haake	2008	Trevor Shirk
1972	Stephen Main	1985	Oliver Alt	1995	Ernest Napier	2009	Micah Lockhart
1973	Charles Hutzler	1985	Christopher Burgin	1995	Clyde Collins	2010	Keri Anderson
1974	Gary Johnsen	1985	Christopher Franks	1995	Michael Greenberg	2010	Jacob Haag
1974	Larry Milam	1986	Mark Coets	1996	John Frick	2012	Harrison Mann
1974	Dean Russell	1987	Leonard Kortekaas	1996	Ian Llewellyn		
1974	John Sladky	1988	Curtis Paarmann	1997	Amanda May-Coussoule		

The Hannibal Trophy

Mule Rider Nels Estvold, Class of 2013, receiving the inaugural Hannibal Award from Sherry and Peter Cashman, owners of the Morgan Farm Stables, the home of the West Point mules.

The Hannibal Trophy is awarded annually for Loyalty.

CHAPTER FIVE

Mule Stories

Hannibal (L) Pancho (R)
1953 West Point
George Perrin '54 (L)
Bob Chapman '54 (C)
Jan LeCroy '54 (R)

Hannibal and Pancho

Walter Price—Army Navy 1949

The following is directly from email correspondence received from Walter Price:

Army/Navy 1949 (Army 38-Navy 0). Rex Jennings, Ralph Stephenson, and myself were the three Mule Riders and I must tell you we were great!! We went to Philadelphia Friday afternoon with Hannibal and Poncho in a large truck with enlisted staff from veterinary detachment. Went to stadium for practice and briefing by Secret Service as to where we could ride in vicinity of President. In those days, no closed boxes—President sat right down next to the field. The President crossed field at half to sit with other Academy.

Cheerleaders found out that at a previous game, Margaret Truman told her Dad she would not switch as she preferred to stay with the Army. The cheerleaders got permission to present Margaret with an Army pendant, which they did at the game on Saturday. The big game plan was to seal the Mules, riders and a cadet to operate a smoke device in a huge "Trojan Mule" and enter the stadium with smoke coming out of the mule nose and have me and Hannibal break out on the Army side (in front of President Truman). We had to be sealed in the container several hours before kickoff. As an aside…if you ever see a picture of Hannibal at that game you'll notice only three hooves are painted gold. We normally painted the hooves before we entered the field but things were so chaotic we couldn't keep Hannibal calm enough to paint all four. With the cramped quarters, noise from smoke machine, etc., etc., Hannibal (normally easy to handle) was acting like a mule. When the ramp dropped I was unable to mount, but did hang on to the reins, mount, and raced through the restricted zone in front of President Truman. The President understood about mules and the Secret Service didn't shoot me!! I raced over to the Navy side and did a trick where I flipped into the air, spun around and landed backwards on Hannibal. Actually Ralph Stevenson was better than I was at this trick…but I had a reason for doing it (details later).

While I was in mid air the Middies charged that damned goat at Hannibal and he did some kind of a gyration, threw me, and one hoof landed on my hand. I had the unique experience of being laughed at by 102,000 people—possibly a record! My hand (barely scratched) started to bleed and laughs changed to "oohs" and "aahs." Being a trained show off I jumped back on Hannibal and rode off in glory as did the greatest team Army ever put on the field.*

*I've almost lost this message as I'm poor at the computer, so I'll send it and then send one telling you why I wanted to show off in front of the Navy stand.

Walter Price-REASON WHY I WANTED TO DO THE TRICK IN FRONT OF NAVY STANDS

After rehearsal at stadium, we were free to "Do Philadelphia"—til early next day at stadium. We (not sure if we were all three together but I know Rex and I were) met some young ladies waiting for their Middie dates the next day. They were charmed by us and why waste an evening? So we did Philadelphia together. Doubt if the Middies got a complete report! At some point my "date" asked me why we were down to Philly early. I told her why and she did not believe me. I told her to watch for me on Hannibal the next day and I'd do a special trick for her. And that's the story.[25]

    – Walter Price

Hannibal (L) Poncho (R)
1949
Ralph Stephenson '50
John Jennings '50 (M-2)
Walter Price '50

CHEERLEADERS
AND MULERIDERS

Adding color to the Big Rabble's victories on the gridiron and leading the Corps' cheers and songs, the cheerleaders and the muleriders did a job equal to the team on the field. Rallies in the Mess Hall and after taps plus stunts at games made this the year of great football and great spirit.

Hannibal
1959 Michie Stadium
Ron Hines (L)
Rod Granneman '61 (L-C)
Mike Fields '60 (R-C)
Bulldog Drennen '60 (R)

Trotter
1964 Michie Stadium
James H. Hall '65
W/Duke Cheerleader

Trotter (L) Hannibal (R)
1960 Location?
Rod Granneman '61
W/Duke? Cheerleader

Ambassador Al Hoffman, Class of 1956

Skippy and Hannibal

We had Mr. Jackson at the time. Mr. Jackson was retired though and stayed in the barn. We had Hannibal and Venezuelan donkey given to us when the Ambassador of Venezuela visited West Point. His name was Skippy. That donkey was the only way we could get Hannibal to go anywhere. We needed Skippy to get him on or off the van, in and out of the stadium. Someone always had to ride Skippy in first to get Hannibal to go in, but man, Hannibal was hell bent for leather once he got to the stadium.[26]

Gymnastics and the Army "A"

Back then, we rode with just a girth with a couple handles. We'd bring two mules to each game but really only used one. We would vault off the mule on one side and do shoulder flips over his withers. Often times, we would mount the mule running up the rear while the other would hold the mule with his reins facing forward. We would just vault up onto him from behind. The crowds really loved it. We tried riding standing on the mule if the mule was in good form and you were feeling extra brave. Well, kind of kneeling/standing. We had a lot of fun. I claim the invention to putting the A on the horses' rumps. When we trimmed the mule, why we would leave out the A impression and that would be long and we would hydrogen peroxide the A so it was gold. I don't know how they do it nowadays but back when I was there that's how we did it.[27]

The mules also wore costumes and were part of elaborate tricks from time to time.

Mr Jackson
1940
Bob Brinson '41 (Top)
Jack Kelsey '41 (Below)

Over the years, many riders did various tricks and gymnastics aboard the mules—often for the attention of a special lady (or two!)

Presidents and Mules

From Steve Townes:

That's me in the plaid Rabble Rouser pants at JFK Stadium in Philadelphia, Army–Navy Game, 1000 years ago. President Ford on the right. I met both Ford and Nixon via the mules. The year before, I was riding the mule when President Nixon came across the field at half-time in the cadet cordon. I reached into my parka pocket for my little Kodak Instamatic camera to snap a photo over the mule's head toward the President, and a VERY strong hand came out of nowhere, grabbed my wrist, and said "Slowly pull your hand out of your pocket." It was a female Secret Service agent! I showed her the camera, then took a photo of President Nixon. It may have been a little bit out of focus, SINCE MY HANDS WERE STILL SHAKING![28]

Big Trouble in the Big House

The following story is from Steve Townes:

One incident was very memorable. You know we rode these mules with a simple snaffle, which is not very strong and for some reason the sergeant said that army regulations forbid using a stronger bit. Hannibal had a way of running away with you. He'd bite it and go. You'd have to try and turn him into a big circle to stop him when he took off.

One time, the Army was going to the Michigan game in Ann Arbor, I ran out to near the plane and asked the general. I said, General, don't you think we oughta take the mascot with us? Sure enough he was able to get a railroad car with a box stall in it and we took Skippy and Hannibal. Fitz Chrysler was the athletic director at the time. He wouldn't let them on the field because he was afraid they'd churn the field up. We were restricted to the sidelines. The mule and the donkey were led into the stadium. The mule took off and ran across the field. He got panicked I guess, and headed straight to the end zone. The students and cadets cheered. Finally, the mule just sat down on his haunches, pulled up a 10–15 foot of sod. Fitz saw it and sent word over to take those mules off and keep them off. We had to essentially standoff and get off the field. The com came off and said you guys gotta get off. We tore off a nice piece of sod for the Michigan people. (1955 maybe, think Army won)[29]

The First Army Mule v. Navy Goat Showdown

Legend has it that in 1899 Navy was bringing their goat to the Army–Navy showdown. Army couldn't show up without a mascot, so they brought a mule. At the first meeting of the Army mule and the Navy goat, neither animal wanted much to do with one another. The Army mule turned around and kicked the Navy goat clear into the stands. But the mule didn't stop there; immediately after, in front of a crowd of 25,000 in Philadelphia, the Army mule laughed at the goat. For anyone who has ever heard the noise that a mule makes, this story is for sure believable. Mules that are pleased make a laughing noise that is a combination of braying and whinnying.

How the cadets acquired the mule remains a mystery. Some say that the mule was purchased from a local man delivering ice. Others say that he was stolen. Personally, I'd bet he was stolen. "Big White" helped the Black Knights win 17–5 in Philadelphia in their first fight on neutral ground. It is unclear if there was another mule until 1936. In 1936, Mr. Jackson came to West Point as the first official mascot of the United States Military Academy.

The first Army-Navy game was played in 1890 on "The Plain." Navy won 24–0 (probably because we didn't have a mascot). This sort of bad luck eventually contributed to the 14-game losing streak leading up the Year of the Mule in 2015. Actually, according to the Chinese calendar, 2015 was the year of the goat, but that was the last year they would win at football against Army for a while.

Raider gets acquainted with the Navy Goat.

In the photo above, General Scott takes a spin on Raider. One of Raider's companions, General Scott is named for him.

Modern Army Navy Meetings

Today, Army–Navy pranks and meetings between goats and mules and mascots and graduates continue.

Kabul, Afghanistan (Dec. 11, 2010). General David H. Petraeus, center, commander of the NATO International Security Assistance Force (IASF) and U.S. Forces Afghanistan, watches a staff member, right, remove a goat adorned with a Navy flag during his morning meeting. Vice Admiral Robert S. Harward, commander of the Combine Joint Interagency Task Force 435, dispatched four sailors to give the general the goat, the U.S. Naval Academy mascot, before the Army–Navy football game in Philadelphia. (U.S. Air Force photo Master Sgt. Adam M. Stump. Caption U.S. Navy.)[30]

Great Mule Caper

Prior to the 1991 Army–Navy football game, the Army mules went undercover. After numerous successful kidnappings of the Navy goat, the Army mules began to get concerned that the Navy goats may have gathered critical intel. The Army mules put their heads together and came up with a plan. They would infiltrate the Midshipmen's headquarters and gather intel themselves! The mules went missing and a multi-state manhunt ensued. The mules were recovered at the gates of Annapolis. They were unharmed but were unable to gather intel since they didn't make it into Annapolis.

The newspapers reported a Great Mule Caper and applauded the story of the 17 midshipmen who used SEAL-type maneuvering and strategy to evade dozens of West Point officers and personnel to kidnap the mules. But... considering the mules' shenanigans, smarts, and loyalty, maybe it was an inside job?

In actuality, this was one of the greatest college pranks of all time. Imagine the logistics of kidnapping a mule! The 17 midshipmen who kidnapped the mules are likely remembered by all midshipmen as heroes for their incredible caper. They're the only people to pull off a mule-napping. There have been no mules kidnapped since.

Actually, the mules were successfully kidnapped prior to the 1991 game-the result of planning one year in the making. Given the central location of the mules at the time, this was particularly impressive. Adding further insult, Army had to first catch their mules who had been turned loose in a field, then listen to the Navy chants at the game, and finally lost the game.[31]

The 1953 Kidnapping of the Navy Goat

Abstracted from Ben Schemmer's eulogy:

The Army Football Team has been upset by the Navy in 1950 and then the Army team was decimated by the subsequent cheating scandal in the summer of 1951. Army lost in 1951 and 1952. So where was Ben in the fall of 1953 as army's football fortunes began to rise? He was the cheerleader in action. He managed the kidnapping of the Navy's mascot, the goat, in a commando type raid at Annapolis and brought it to West Point. I doubt that anyone who was there will forget that Sunday dinner when huge plywood boards were pulled away from the PT stand in the middle of Washington Hall. There stood Ben and that goat. Magnificent! Pandemonium. Spirit zoomed, and isn't that what cheerleaders are for?

While the cadets were delighted and excited, the academy administration was alarmed and stern. The plan had been to return the goat to the Navy in Philadelphia at the Army–Navy Game the subsequent Saturday. But the Tactical Department ordered that the goat be returned to Annapolis immediately. This order caused disorder and a great demonstration vigorously led by Ben in the Central Area in front of the Headquarters of the Tactical Department. (This event was headlined in one New York Newspaper as "Goat Rebellion at West Point?") But where was the goat? Once the Cadets were in classes for the afternoon and to avoid any honor violations or further disciplinary actions, the goat's location was revealed. Wisely the kidnappers had placed the goat in the hands of the Post Veterinarian to avoid any charges that this animal was being maltreated. Some poor Tactical Officer whose name escapes me, but probably rather juniors had the task of returning the goat to Annapolis. For Ben's spirited actions, he was demoted to Private and transferred from L-2 to (oh horrors!) B-1. So, of course, Army won the game.

The fact of the matter is that Ben was on the brink of expulsion from the military academy. But a young Tactical Officer, a captain, spoke up at the Disciplinary Committee hearing and defended Ben. Reduction in rank and transfer from L-2 was considered adequate punishment. Years later in his autobiography, that General—then Captain Alexander M. Haig—stated that

Ben was just the sort of officer he would want in his unit and expulsion was not in the best interests of the service. His view prevailed.[32]

Kid-Napping

After several instances of mascot-napping, Academy leadership at all Academies has cracked down on mascot-napping. Will it last?

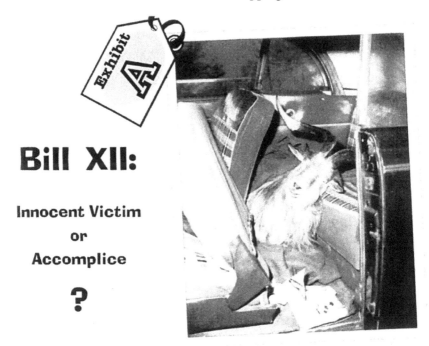

Navy Goat 2, 22 Nov 1953

Steve Townes, Class of 1975

Let me tell about the time I was almost expelled from the Academy. We were out in Colorado for the Air Force Football Game. I don't remember when it was in the game but it was late when we were just miserably losing. I rode the mule over slowly to the Air Force side. As I rode it over, here came a coke cup hurling down out of the crowd, probably still had some ice in it. It was heavy enough to throw. Hit the mule smack in the head. The mule jumped up, did a lone ranger stance, almost threw me. I looked up in the crowd and I saw the guy that did it. I looked up and I pointed at him. Then I did something bad. I had black gloves and black button up cardigan with a golden A on it. I slipped most of the fingers into the cardigan minus the middle finger. I was essentially flipping him the bird but not. I told all the other rabble rousers about it and they said, "Wow, good thing you kept control."

Back at West Point, maybe that Thursday, I got a call from thecommandant's aide, captain Pratt, and he said General Feir (Yea, Fear. He used to say you have nothing to fear but Feir himself) would like to see you. He said, "Mr. Townes, you better put on your best shoes and get a haircut." I said, "Captain Pratt, what is this in regards to?" He said, "I don't know but you better get here."

I got to the office and the aide just looked me up and down, not helping my nerves. I was called into General Feir's office. He kept me standing at a full salute at his desk for a full thirty seconds while he glared before he returned the salute and said, "You know why you're here."

I said, "No sir."

He picked up a folder and tossed it across the desk. An 8 × 10 photo was in that folder. He pointed at that picture and said, "That's why you're here."

The photograph was sent with a nasty note from General VanderBerg, Superintendent of the Air Force Academy. The note said something like, "You better burn this kid."

I was shaking in my boots. I was thinking I am about to be dismissed. I owned it. "Here are the facts. I did it, yes sir, it was me, I did that, but I thought he could have put the mule's eye out, the mules could have back-kicked and hurt someone, and there were people there."

I bravely continued on with my justification of my mature handling of the situation. "Frankly, I'm glad I did it that way instead of raising my fist and flipping him the bird."

The General just sat there. Then he said, "All things considered, would you do it again?"

He continued to sit there silent with those ice-cold blue laser eyes were boring through me like darts as I replied "Yes."

He then asked me, "What do you think I should do about this?"

My reply was, "You're the commandant of cadets, sir. You can do what you want. But I would have done it again."

He said give me that photograph, got a marker out, and said, "Here, sign it so we can send it back to him good and proper.

As I was leaving I saw that Captain Pratt and the General's Secretary were in the doorway listening and laughing the whole time. They were both in on this as I was sitting there literally with sweat running down my neck thinking I was getting kicked out! I don't know what happened to that photo but I hope it's there at the Air Force Academy somewhere. As it turns out General Feir and General VanderBerg were roommates back in their football days in West Point! The whole thing had just been funny to both of them and funny to me now, decades later, having graduated from West Point.[33]

Story from Steve Townes, Class of 1975

Be tactful with this one. The only way to describe it is gaucheness. Being the friendly gentlemen we were, at football games, we'd go to the other side of the stadium and offer to the cheerleaders, "Would you like to ride the mule?" They'd always say yes, and we'd help them up, pulling them up onto the mule. We would ride them around the stadium, take them to the other side, let them wave at their fans. Everyone would cheer and love it. Most nights, I'd get a date out of it. I'm not saying I was using mules to pick up chicks but literally I was picking them up! And that's how it went. It wasn't the primary objective. The primary objective was to support the football team, team spirit, etc., and of course the mules. Certainly a secondary dividend was dates with the cheerleaders that evening.

After a little time of riding around with the cheerleaders on the back of the mules, a new chant started. They'd start chanting, pass her up. The corps were all male at that time. "Passing her up" meant they'd send the ladies up hand-over-hand; they wanted her to lay flat and get passed up, like a log if you will all the way up and all the way down. We'd do it quite often, they'd typically come down and hop right back on the mule, maybe a little disheveled and maybe a little bit blushing but always in good humor, but everyone always seemed to have a good time with it. "Pass her up" was a chant in the 70s with the mules, as we'd offer up their cheerleaders almost as a tribute. I think in our yearbook there was a picture or two with their hair flying in all directions with the corps passing them up. The cheerleaders liked being able to ride on the mules and get passed back up. I remember one gal's reactions as behind me going "Woo! Man!"[34]

When Hell Froze Over in Colorado-Famous Mules and Myths

As stated earlier, mules can't reproduce. They are sterile. There have been a handful of mules that have allegedly reproduced foals, but none were verified until 2007, when a mule named Kate gave birth. The baby, Kule Mule Amos, lived to be three years old.

The Denver Post reported on the birth of Kule Mule Amos in 2007 and again in 2013, three years after the death of the youngster. The day that the Denver Post reported on it, it was the top-read story with over 67,000 clicks in three days. The youngster was named by the public that voted on it.

Horses have 64 chromosomes and donkeys have 62 chromosomes. Mules are born with 63 chromosomes. Since they can't be split evenly, they can't reproduce. Somehow Kule Mule had a mix of cells that were 64 and 62 chromosomes. Unfortunately the little guy had malformed legs and health problems. His life was short but he was well loved, his family claimed in the Denver Post article.[35]

In the past, mules giving birth have been reported and panic has ensued. Ancient Romans had a phrase, "cum mula peperit," meaning "when a mule foals." This is our equivalent to saying "when hell freezes over" or "when pigs fly." It was so unlikely that a mule would ever give birth that the ancient Romans used it to describe improbable circumstances. Ancient people believed in many superstitions. One of which was the birth of a mule as a bad omen. It was such an unnatural and unlikely event that it was said to predict bad fortune.[36]

In Histories by Herodotus, he recorded Xerxes' invasion of Greece in 480 B.C. The invasion was an utter disaster and was attributed in part to Xerxes ignoring the birth of the mule and other omens foretelling of disaster.[37]

In Albania in 1994, a mule's foal was thought to have unleashed a spawn of the devil on the small village; and in 2002 in Morocco, locals thought it was the signal of the end of the world.

Poncho (L) Hannibal (R)
1956 Howze Field
George O'Grady '57
Don Bowman '57

Hannibal(L) Pancho(R)
1955 Michie Stadium
Paul "Woody" Hayne III '56
Al Hoffman, Jr '56

CHAPTER SIX

Goats and Falcons

Bill, the Goat

Because every protagonist needs an antagonist....From the United States Naval Academy.

"Long before midshipmen began tossing the pigskin around the site of old Fort Severn, goats were an integral part of Navy life. Over 200 years ago, livestock was kept aboard some seagoing naval vessels to provide sailors with food, milk, eggs and, in some cases, pets.

One legend about the first association of the goat with Navy football tells of a pet goat who died at sea while on board a Navy ship. The affection for the goat was such that the officers decided to save the skin of the animal and have it mounted upon arrival in port.

Two young officers were entrusted with the skin when the ship docked in Baltimore. On the way to the taxidermist, the ensigns dropped in on their alma mater, where a football game was in progress. With them—for lack of a suitable storage place—was the goat skin.

While watching the first half of the game, one of the officers came up with an idea for some half-time entertainment. When half-time arrived, he romped up and down the sidelines cloaked with the goat skin barely covering his blue uniform. Such un-goat-like antics brought howls of laughter from the midshipmen, and the Navy victory that day was attributed to the spirit of the late, lamented goat.

It was not until 1893, however, that a live goat made his debut as a mascot at the fourth Army–Navy game. Again, it was young naval officers who supplied the mids with their seafaring pet. The USS New York dropped anchor off Annapolis and the ship's mascot, a goat bearing the name El Cid (the Chief), was brought ashore for the service clash. The West Pointers were defeated for the third time, and the midshipmen feted El Cid along with the team.

According to the United States Naval Academy Public Affairs Office, the first service match of the 20th century brought out both teams' traditional mascots for the first time. The mids again borrowed the goat from the USS New York and decked him out in a fine blanket with a gold "NAVY" emblazoned on both sides. On the opposite side of the gridiron, the Army mule was attired in West Point colors and bore on one side the words "No Ships for Me" while on the other flank was "I'm Something of a Kicker Myself."

That game in Philadelphia ended with an 11–7 victory for Annapolis and added prestige for the goat. On the return trip to the Naval Academy, the goat was led on a victory lap through the train and did not leave the mids until they reached Baltimore. It was then that the goat was dubbed the now-celebrated name "Bill." The name was borrowed from a pet goat kept by Commander Colby M. Chester, Commandant of Midshipmen from 1891 to 1894 and the first president of the Naval Academy Athletic Association.

The next year a new goat, named Bill II, was called upon to assume the role of Navy mascot. Along with him, however, were two easily spooked cats who ran for the nearest exit when released from their bag. Navy lost again and goat advocates protested against the joint attention the cats received.

In 1905, the fifth goat, a large angora animal from Princeton, New Jersey, was given the name of Bill III and bestowed with the duty of bringing victory to the Navy, who had lost the last four years to Army. That year the teams deadlocked 6–6.

The following year, another goat wore the blanket, and it was this mascot which was destined for fame. Originally called Bill, this goat was dubbed "Three-to-Nothing Jack Dalton," after the star midshipman who kicked the field goals that helped Navy defeat Army 3–0 for two successive years.

In 1912, plans were made to honor the goat that had acted as mascot for the previous seven years. Late in November, "Jack" was measured for a new blue-and-gold blanket, but one week later (November 20) he was stricken with colic and dead.

Elaborate plans were made for a funeral, but it was decided instead to have his skin mounted. "Three-to-Nothing Jack Dalton" can be seen today in the foyer of the Academy's Halsey Field House, mounted in a glass case, reared on his hind legs in a fighting pose.

A brown goat was enlisted into mascot service in 1914, and his wicked temper earned him the name of Satan. Luck seemed to be on Satan's side, as he was the only goat allowed out of the state during a livestock quarantine to attend the Army–Navy game in Philadelphia. But Satan's luck was short-lived, and disgrace was heaped upon him when his esteemed blanket was taken away after Navy's defeat that year.

Finding a goat that could bring victory over Army was beginning to look like an impossible task. To solve this problem, the following ad was run in an Annapolis newspaper in 1916: "WANTED: the meanest and fiercest goat possible...Would like to see same before purchasing."

Navy got what it wanted: a mean goat and a victory over Army. He was called Bill VI.

A later goat, Bill VIII was a large, white goat with a wicked eye. With horns painted blue and gold, the goat went to New York for the West Point contest. Given every amenity to insure victory, he was given an entire room filled with straw on the twenty-second floor of a hotel. Bill victoriously returned to Annapolis with the mule's blanket and remained with Navy for several more seasons. After World War II, the Navy turned to an angora named, "Chester" for goatly guidance. Named after Admiral Chester W. Nimitz, the midshipmen changed the mascot's name to Bill XIII. Rather ominously, he died on the eve of the 1947 game with Army.

His successor, Bill XIV, was presented during the emergency by an Annapolis barber. A loyal mascot, Bill XIV was a frequent target of kidnapping by rival schools. Another of the Navy's famed goats, he had a 5–5–2 record over Army and a twelve-year reign, the longest of all previous goat mascots.

Since that time there have been a number of goats who served as the honored mascot of the Academy, and several of them have unusual stories.

In 1968 Bill XVI, a gift from the Air Force Academy, died of accidental poisoning from weed killer sprayed too closely to his pen.

His successor, Bill XVII, met the same fate three years later.

Bill XIX and Bill XX died of natural causes after each served three years of faithful service, in 1975 and 1978, respectively.

Bill XXI led the midshipmen to their best record in years, which included a 23–16 victory over Brigham Young University in the 1978 Holiday

Bowl. He is also credited with two Navy wins over Army, which then brought the competition to 37 wins apiece for the two archrivals.

Bill XXXIII and Bill XXXIV retired in 2015. Bill XXXV died in August, 2016.

The current Academy mascots are Bill XXXVI and Bill XXXVII. They are taken care of by 15 goat handlers made up of five midshipmen from the first, second, and third classes. The goat handlers undergo rigorous training prior to handling Bill on the field.

Two cats, a dog, and a carrier pigeon have also enjoyed brief reigns as the Navy mascot, but goats have served without interruption since 1904."[38]

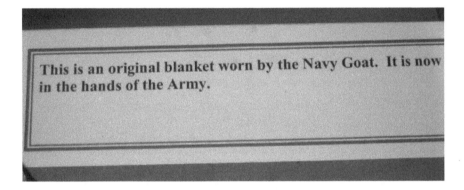

This is an original blanket worn by the Navy Goat. It is now in the hands of the Army.

The cadets and the midshipmen at each Army–Navy football game used to bring the animals to meet one another at the beginning of the game and at the end, and the losing animal had to give their blanket to the winning team.

These photographs are of the Navy goat's blanket that was forfeited to the Army Black Knights after a victory over Navy.

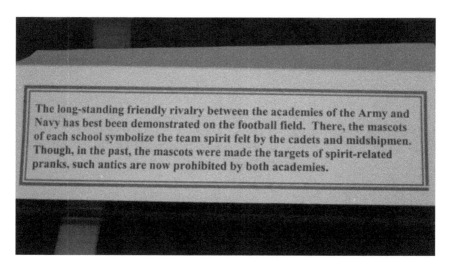

The long-standing friendly rivalry between the academies of the Army and Navy has best been demonstrated on the football field. There, the mascots of each school symbolize the team spirit felt by the cadets and midshipmen. Though, in the past, the mascots were made the targets of spirit-related pranks, such antics are now prohibited by both academies.

Although everyone agrees that the pranks should not be reinstated at the Academies, the blanket forfeiture to the winning team is an old tradition that ought to be reinstated.

The Air Force Falcon

The Air Force falcon, in this author's opinion, has the least amount of fanfare. A search on the Air Force website will yield very few photos and information, if any. The falcon mascot was selected by popular vote of the Academy's Class of 1959, the first class to graduate from the Academy. The team mascot is "Mach 1," name of the first falcon presented to the academy on October 5, 1955; however, each performing falcon is given an individual name by its cadet falconer. The longest-serving mascot was a female white-phase gyrfalcon named Aurora, which was the official mascot since 1996. Aurora passed away in 2019 after a 2018 injury during a prank abduction by West Point cadets. Current falcons are Ziva, Zeus, Oblio, Nova, Karena, Cairo, Apollo, and Ace.[39]

The Air Force Falcon meets Ranger III who keeps a suspicious eye on the bird at Michie Stadium

CHAPTER SEVEN

West Point Support

*The mule riders with Ranger II and Raider in Philadelphia for the 2010
Army-Navy football game. This was Ranger II and Raider's last trip
to Philadelphia.*

The Mule Endowment

Steve Townes is mentioned often in this book as he's the man who introduced me to all of the other mule aficionados! Mr. Townes is not only a former rabble rouser and successful graduate of West Point but he is owed a tremendous amount of gratitude for the mules. When the Hannibal monument was dedicated in 2004, Mr. Townes stated that the mules needed proper upkeep, tack, and so on, and committed to a permanent endowment. A requirement of the endowment is that one mule is always named Ranger in honor of the Army Rangers. Ranger II was serving at that time, and the Academy has kept their end of the bargain, Ranger III now serves West Point.

How to Keep the Army Mules in Top Shape

The Army Mules have to not just be kept in top shape because they're athletes but also because they represent the traditions of the United States Army.

First, the mules have to be conditioned. The official conditioning program of the Army Mules is Classified. Actually, it isn't, but it's always changing and varies based on the animals.

Mules need less conditioning than horses. A horse will eat and eat and eat to the point where it can jeopardize the horse's health. A mule will stop eating when it is full.

Mule riders at West Point are selected from each class. They care for the mules and condition the mules. The mules need to not only be athletic and able to perform their duties as sturdy mounts for their cadets, but must also be able to interact with children, elderly, disabled, over-zealous tailgaters, and everyone in between.

The mules are ambassadors and must behave appropriately. They must also not become upset with distractions such as crowds or even cannons. This requires a lot of time and effort spent to help them become acquainted with things that would normally upset another horse or mule.

Grooming the Mules

Grooming the mules can be tricky business. They must be maintained constantly, not just for appearances but for their own comfort. As the hair grows out, the mule is bothered and itchy. Once the "A" grows out, it is more difficult to place it. The Clairol Basic White pictured below works the best to dye the hair.

Below is a piece from the Mule Museum describing the process of putting the "A's" on the mules. The mule pictured is Raider.

Cadets saddling and getting the mules ready for the Army Navy Game. Note their hooves are painted black. The As are shaved and dyed. They have special army saddles and bridles.

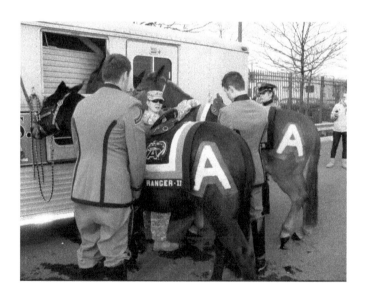

The cadets have traditional English riding boots and spurs on. The mules have custom Army saddle blankets and halters with their names on them.

These photos were taken at the 2010 Army Navy game in Philadelphia. Their hooves are painted so their shoes shine like any fine Army Officer's should!

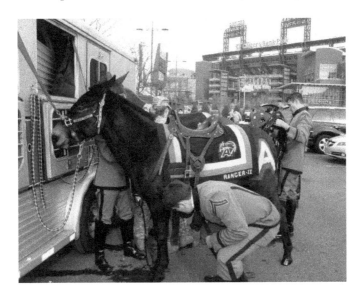

Mule Tack

Mules can participate in every discipline that a horse can and then some. The Army Field Manual 3-05.213, Special Forces Use of Pack Animals has several saddles and bridles in it, shown on the following pages.

The Field Manual serves Special Forces Soldiers and Units all over the world when interacting with pack animals. Many of those soldiers have never interacted with a pack animal prior to their service. The Field Manual contains many illustrations of tack.

As seen in the photographs of the mules, many different mules wore different tack. Different equipment may be more advantageous for different condition.

Raider, Ranger II, and General Scott primarily wore the McClellan saddle pictured below.

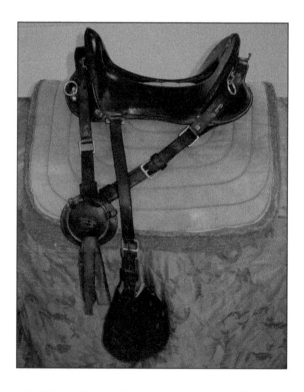

Army Field Manual 3-05.213, Special Forces Use of Pack Animals,
Figure 6-5, McClellan Saddle

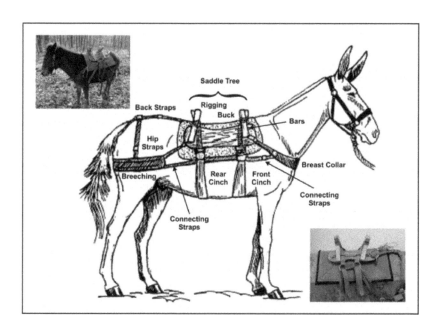

Army Field Manual 3-05.213, Special Forces Use of Pack Animals, Figure 5-1, Sawbuck Saddle on a Mule

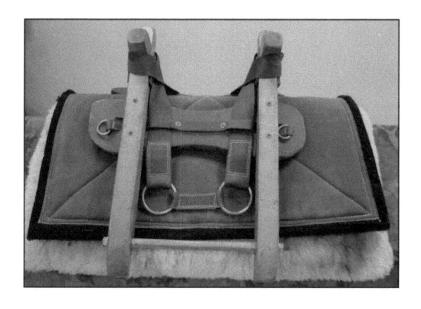

Army Field Manual 3-05.213, Special Forces Use of Pack Animals, Figure 5-2, Bradshaw Saddle

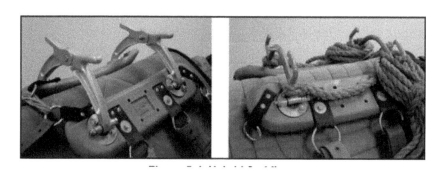

Army Field Manual 3-05.213, Special Forces Use of Pack Animals, Figure 5-3 Decker Saddle with Half-Breed Saddle Cover and Army Field Manual 3-05.213, Special Forces Use of Pack Animals Figure 5-4 Hybrid Saddles

Army Field Manual 3-05.213, Special Forces Use of Pack Animals,
Figure 6-1. Typical Horse Bridle and Standard Bit

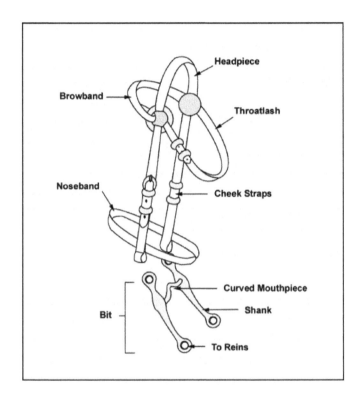

Army Field Manual 3-05.213, Special Forces Use of Pack Animals, Figure 6-3, Western Saddles

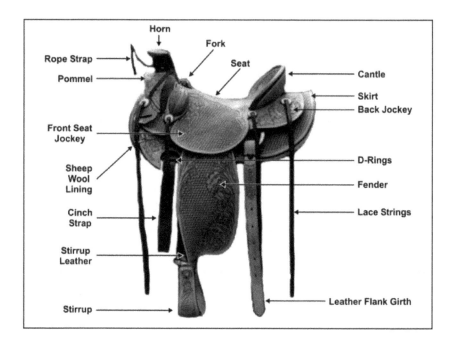

"Beat Navy" is shown on a lot of pieces of Army Mule Tack. These pictures show a rabies tag issued at the veterinary clinic at West Point.

 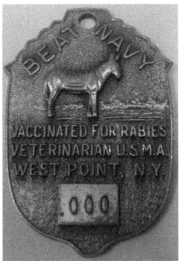

The mules travel in style in their three-horse trailer. They're easy to spot when they are on the move in the U.S. Military Academy trailer. Their names are printed below their windows, so that their fans know who is who when they're interacting with their adoring crowds.

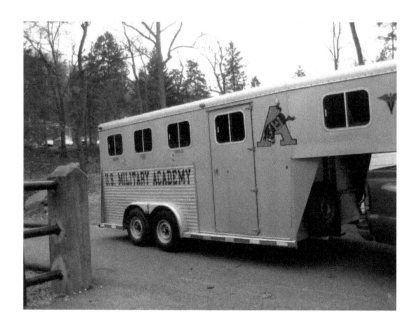

The mules are some of the best dressed members of our Armed Forces. In addition to their regular tack, they are often outfitted with special occasion or ceremonial blankets with patches and insignia on them. Or given special tack for special games like the mule leggings, shown on the next page.

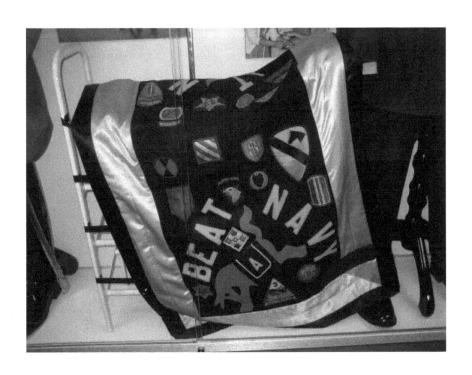

The Johnson Veterinary Facility

"The West Point mules move around from time to time. They currently live at Morgan Farm outside the main gate of West Point. Previously, they lived at the heart of the reservation at the Johnson Veterinary Facility. The Johnson Veterinary Facility is named after Sergeant First Class Robert P. Johnson. SFC Robert P. Johnson served the Corps of Cadets and USMA from 1934 to 1963. A third-generation Buffalo Soldier, he was assigned to the 9th and 10th Cavalry Regiments, where he assisted in Cadet Equestrian Training and Cavalry Escort Duties. When the Cavalry Detachment was disbanded in 1946, he was assigned to the West Point Veterinary and Preventative Medicine Service, where he served for 15 years.

In 1947, he was instrumental in retaining two mules and a donkey to serve as mascots–the beginning of the USMA Mule Mascot Program. After World War II, all equines were banned from West Point. Had it not been for SFC Robert P. Johnson and his efforts to retain the mules, there would be no Army mules today.

118

SFC Johnson's awards include the Good Conduct Model (seventh award), Army Commendation Medal, Korean Service Medal, United Nations Service Medal, World War II Victory Medal, American Defense Service Ribbon, American Campaign Medal, and National Defense Service Ribbon.

Below: Corridor to the Mules at the Veterinary Facility

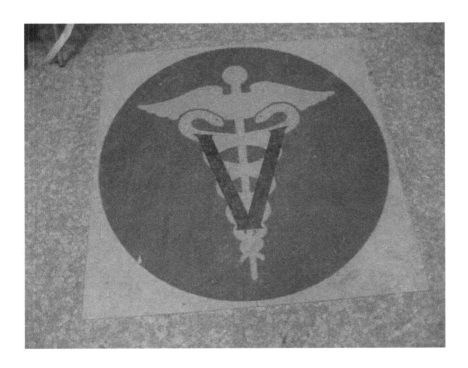

As part of SFC Johnson's funeral service in 1986, a lone mule, Spartacus, led the procession. When the casket was placed, Spartacus let out a long, mournful bray to let all know that his beloved friend and companion had been laid to rest."[40]

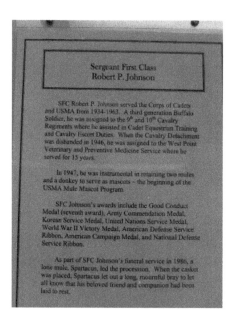

These photographs are tributes at the veterinary facility and the mule museum to SFC Johnson.

The Army Mule Museum at the United States Military Academy holds some of the cherished history of America's mascot. Pictured are some of the commemorative mule items and memorabilia from the years.

Stay tuned for plans to move it when a new equestrian facility is built.

CHAPTER EIGHT

Hannibal (1948-1964)

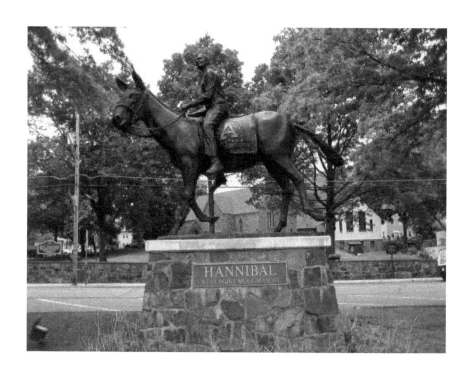

A Tribute to LTC Willis C. 'Tiny" Tomsen, '54

West Point visitors will often make the Hannibal monument their meeting place in Highland Falls. "Meet back at the mule" is often overheard during busy times at the academy. There is a reason for that. His name is Tiny Tomsen.

There has been no greater champion of the West Point mules than Tiny. Since 2004, he has been the individual most responsible for a renewed awareness, support, respect, and reverence for West Point's official and iconic mascot.

His crusade began when Tiny convinced his M-2 company mates to offer a special gift to West Point at their 50th Reunion in 2004. In 2014, he wrote:

"Our mules were famous in movies, books and posters. They were photographed with movie stars, ballplayers and other celebrities. Each year the mules—and the goats—were natural photo subjects of newspapers and magazines nationwide. Everyone knew and loved the West Point mules. Somewhere and somehow our Mules became marginalized and less central as our symbol

"That has changed. Much of that change is due to the leadership and determination to restore the mules to prominence by our Company M-2, Class of 1954. We provided the Hannibal Monument in 2004. It was furthered by the generosity of Steve Townes and others. Then we created the Hannibal Trophy for the Outstanding Mule Rider. There are brighter days ahead for our Army Mules."

After their 50th Reunion, Company M-2 (now Mule 2) gathered again five years later and hosted a birthday party for Hannibal. Tiny arranged for 1,000 mule cookies to be served with "mule punch."

After the Hannibal monument dedication in 2004, Tiny started another crusade to make the Army "A" with a kicking mule a universal icon for West Point. He was making progress before he passed away in 2018. It was Tiny's plan to create a large "A" with kicking mule sculpture and place it near north entrance to Michie Stadium near Lusk Reservoir. He envisioned a place where Army fans could congregate and use that monument for photo opportunities.

The Tomsen legacy continues at West Point. His son, Chris, and grandson Erik are both graduates. His M-2 company mates installed a memorial plaque in his honor at the base of the Hannibal monument.

Tiny Tomsen is buried in the West Point Cemetery. West Point's three active mules and their riders stood sentinel at his service.[41]

A mockup of the proposed "Kicking A" statue is pictured above.

Walter Price, Hannibal's First Rider by Mike Lapolla

Walter Price rode Mr. Jackson, West Point's first official mule—and Hannibal I, West Point's most storied one.

LTC (Ret.) Walter Price was Class of 1950, and likely West Point's most fortunate and colorful mule rider. West Point's first named mule was Mr. Jackson (1936-48). The most celebrated mule is Hannibal (1948-64). On September 24, 1949, a Michie Stadium ceremony retired Mr. Jackson and introduced Hannibal. Walter trained Hannibal for the prior year and was his first rider. And Walter rode Mr. Jackson during the retirement ceremony. His high school classmate Rex Jennings, was also one of the three mule riders in the ceremony.

He served as an enlisted man during WWII, then entered West Point in 1946. During Walter's military career as an Infantry Officer, he served in Korea and Vietnam, and was a West Point Professor of Military Psychology and Leadership . He is a member of the highly selective Oklahoma Military Hall of Fame and the Oklahoma Military Academy Hall of Fame.[42]

Pictured above in March, 2004 at the OK Founder's Day is Hannibal with Tiny Tomsen, and Walter & Jane Price.. The monument was dedicated two months later at Highland Falls.

Meet Me At The Mule

According to Tiny Tomsen, West Point Class of 1954, "Mules have a long and wonderful history in the U.S. Army." Yet there was not a monument dedicated to the mules. When Mr. Tomsen contacted West Point to donate a mule statue, they turned him down. He had one cast anyway. Mr. Tomsen raised and contributed to the fund to cover the $125,000 expense for the mule statue. A 15-foot mule statue now stands in Highland Falls, New York, just across from the West Point visitors center. Although West Point refused the statue, Highland Falls was more than happy to accept it. Rumor has it the superintendent at the time refused the statue, but at least one subsequent superintendent has asked the city to donate the statue to West Point, which Highland Falls has understandably refused to do. Below are photos of Big Bertha.

Big Bertha

The statue was sculpted by J. David Nunneley of Broken Arrow, Oklahoma. It is sculpted in the likeness of Hannibal. When Mr. Nunneley was contacted he didn't know much about mules. That all changed in a flash!

Mr. Nunneley and Tiny visited West Point and got all the paraphernalia from Hannibal's time. He and Tiny visited a Claremore, Oklahoma mule farm and located Big Bertha, the mule that looked the most similar to Hannibal to use for inspiration. Mr. Nunneley measured him and rode him. He then went to Colorado and learned more about mules, falling in love with them. He selected a pose agreeable to Tiny and made a small maquette, mock-up model. The actual sculpting took about 6 months before sending the sculpture to the foundry. The whole process took about two years.

An inscription on the statue reads: "Since 1899 the mule has been the West Point mascot promoting the spirit of the Corps of Cadets. Mules were very important to the Army in the late 1800s through World War I. While not regular cavalry mounts, mules were used extensively to pull supply wagons, caissons, and artillery pieces. Mules are stronger, more surefooted, more intelligent, and eat less than horses."

The monument was dedicated on May 22, 2004. In 2009, the class of 1954 met to celebrate its 55th anniversary and visit Hannibal. Hannibal was wished a happy fifth birthday!

Over three million people pass by the Hannibal statue each year. Because of the Hannibal statue, over three million people are now able to see and appreciate the valuable contribution that the mule has made to the United States Army for centuries.

At West Point, it is often overhead that visitors will make Hannibal their meeting place. "Meet back at the mule" is overheard during busy times at West Point.[43]

One of the original photos of Big Bertha above.

Pictured top: the creation of the Hannibal monument. Pictured Middle: the Monument. Pictured Bottom: Big Bertha and Hannibal the final product of Hannibal.

The drawings for the Hannibal statue.

The programs for the Mule Dedication Ceremony and the 1954 50th Class Reunion are pictured below.

PROGRAM, DEDICATION OF HANNIBAL
11 am Sat, May 22, 2004
Highland Falls, New York

Instrumental Music............James I. O'Neill HS Band
ON BRAVE OLD ARMY TEAM ...." ....

Post the Colors...................Buffalo Soldiers Jr ROTC
Pledge Allegiance............Cadet CSGM Steve Nelson

Welcome.....................W.C. "Tiny" Tomsen M-2 '54

The Bond Between Highland Falls and
            West Point............Mayor Joseph E. D'Onofrio

Unveiling... Head Cadet Mule Rider James Alfaro '05
                    and Highland Falls Officials

Mules and Life are Tough.............. Steve Townes '75

50 Yrs and Forward............Frank Hart '54 President

Recognize M-2 Donors........Jack Beringer M-2 '54

Hannibal, Greatest Mule Ever........... Jan LeCroy '54

Mule Riders Past & Present.........George Perrin '54

Closing Comments.......W.C. "Tiny" Tomsen M-2 '54

MULE PUNCH & MULE COOKIES
Served by Junior Troop 301
Sarah Wells Girl Scout Council

Photos of the inscriptions on the Hannibal monument.

Photos from the Hannibal dedication.

The Unveiling of Hannibal

Highland Falls had the first of many celebrations for the Army mules when the Hannibal statue was unveiled on Saturday, May 22, 2004.

Highland Falls celebrities General Scott, Ranger II, and Raider were on hand for the festivities as they greeted their adoring fans and mule enthusiasts from all over.

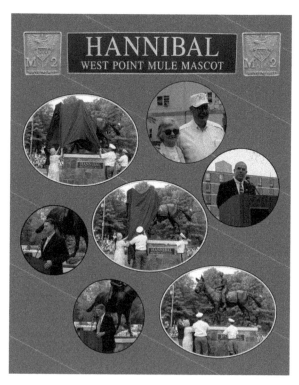

Happy Birthday Hannibal!!

Army mule enthusiasts love any reason to celebrate. The dedication of the Army mule statue was filled with all of the pomp and circumstance that the Army mules deserve. Army mule fans won't stop there. They also celebrated the fifth anniversary of the mule statue and the tenth anniversary of the mule statue. Hannibal has "birthday" celebrations from time to time that everyone participates in. The current Army mules participate. The people of Highland Falls come out to show their appreciation for the Army mules and often high-ranking officers at West Point join in the celebration. The following pages are from Hannibal's fifth birthday party. Below is the cake from Hannibal's tenth birthday in 2014.

CHAPTER NINE

More Mules

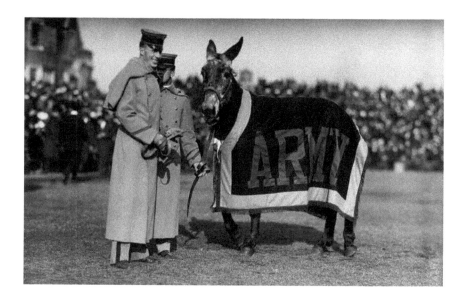

The Mule Fan Club

When picking up Raider and Ranger II from West Point in December, 2011, something adorable happened.

Raider and Ranger II were loaded onto the trailer and a box was given to the man driving them home. The box contained treats and cards that had been given to the mules.

When Ranger II, General Scott, and Raider were at West Point, the mules were housed at the veterinary clinic located near residents of West Point. Local kids often interacted with them.

Raider maintained a soft spot for children and was forever grateful to the kindness shown to him by the West Point kids.[44]

Do all Mules have personalities like the West Point Mule?

Mules are incredibly intelligent and have impeccable memory. This author has spoken with countless people over the years about mules and heard some great stories.

A rather silly story that has not been substantiated but is certainly entertaining is as follows:

In a small town in Wales, there were several working men who used mules. They were always rushed and running up against deadlines. The men would shout and curse at the mules to make them go faster. The men were rough and tough and unsophisticated. They would drink, curse, and womanize when able to. One day, some missionaries really impacted them. The men no longer womanized, drank, or cursed.

When the men tried to tell the mules to pull the wagons, the mules refused to move. The mules only responded to curse words and only curse words could make them go quicker!

All mules have their own personalities. They have their own things that make them tick. They have their favorite people and people they don't care for. Some prefer men, some prefer women. Some can tell when you're afraid and seem to think it's funny when they can exploit this in their human handlers. Some want to be around their human handlers all of the time, and some really need their "alone time." Getting to know any particular mule can take a lot of time, just like getting to know a person, except they can't talk to you!

Other Famous Mules

- Hoopoe, King Solomon's mule
- Jesus the mule is the mayor of Buckskin Joe Frontier Town.
- Swiffy the donkey is an official Democrat Party delegate.
- Francis the Talking Mule needs no description.
- In Biblical times, mules were only ridden by royalty. At Solomon's coronation, he rode a hinny owned by King David.
- Apollo, listed in the Guinness Book of World Records at 19.1 hands. Remember a hand is 4 inches. So, at his withers, Apollo is 77 inches tall!!
- Fanny is the model for Big Ass Fans.
- Duldul (or Fadda in some accounts), the white mule ridden by the prophet Mohammed.
- Ruth on Gunsmoke.

Smoke, the Marine

Much like the Army Mules that serve side by side with their human counter parts, Smoke the donkey served with Marines in Iraq. When Smoke the Marine came back to the United States, he spent the remainder of his life in a therapy program for wounded warriors.[45]

Francis the Talking Mule

Proof that all mules want to be West Point Mules:
Francis the Talking Mule: Proof That All mules Want to Be West Point Mules
Francis, the Talking Mule was a popular series of movies in the 1950s. In 1952, the third Francis movie was produced. The main character is a bumbling idiot that manages to stop a plot to blow up his government workplace. As a reward, he is given the opportunity to attend the United States Military Academy. He is tutored by Francis, his old mule friend. He eventually gets into trouble after revealing that he is being tutored by one of the West Point's mule mascots![46]

Why is the donkey the mascot of the Democrat Party?

The now-famous Democratic donkey was first associated with Democrat Andrew Jackson's 1828 presidential campaign. His opponents called him a jackass, and Jackson decided to use the image of the strong-willed animal on his campaign posters. Later, cartoonist Thomas Nast used the Democratic donkey in newspaper cartoons and made the symbol famous.

Nast invented another famous symbol—the Republican elephant. In a cartoon that appeared in Harper's Weekly in 1874, Nast drew a donkey clothed in lion's skin, scaring away all the animals at the zoo. One of those animals, the elephant, was labeled "The Republican Vote." That's all it took for the elephant to become associated with the Republican Party.

Democrats say the donkey is smart and brave, while Republicans say the elephant is strong and dignified.[47]

Where They Are Now? West Point's Most Famous Mule Riders and Enthusiasts

Al Hoffman, Class of 1956, was Ambassador to Portugal and the CEO of Watermark Communities, Inc., a $4B Company.

Jan LeCroy, Class of 1954, was the founding Chancellor of the eleven-campus Dallas Community Colleges, with 50,000 students.

Steve Townes, Class of 1975, is the founder and CEO of Ranger Aerospace. Townes graduated first in his Ranger School class and served as an officer in the Army 75th Ranger Battalion. Thanks to Mr. Townes' generosity creating the mule endowment, there will always continue to be West Point mules.

Tiny Tomsen, Willis "Tiny" Tomsen passed away June 4, 2018 surrounded by family and friends. He was an Army Lt. Colonel and avid outdoorsman. At West Point he also played football and was the Howitzer photographer. Although not a mule rider, he was responsible for the Hannibal statue.

Mike Lapolla, class of 1965, was born and raised in Peekskill, New York. He left the Army as a Captain in 1973 after two tours in Vietnam. He married his wife Carol in 1967 and they have one son. He resides in Oklahoma and is on the faculty of the University of Oklahoma College of Public Health. Although not a mule rider, he is responsible for much of the assistance with this book and preserving the history of the mule.

KC Mo (L) Trotter (R)
1964 Location?
Bob Kesmodel '66 (L)
James Hall' 65 (R)

Hannibal debuts at the 1949 Army-Navy game, ridden by Cadet Mule Rider Walter Price.

Mr Jackson
1945
Yankee Stadium
John Bartholf '46

CITY CADET RIDES MULE AT ARMY GAMES

Williamsport's Jim Hall, a first classman at West Point, is close to the scene of action at Army's football games. The city cadet rides Trotter, the larger of the two Army mule mascots, at the grid games. Jim, who had never ridden a horse or mule before, had to practice diligently to learn to ride his mule bareback. In his final year at West Point, the 21-year-old Hall has become quite adept at riding. The cadet corps runs from the parade grounds to the stadium prior to the football game and the mules lead the way. During halftime Hall and his companion take their mules to the visitor's side of the field and take the visiting cheerleaders for a ride. At left, Hall and Trotter move along the sideline to follow the action last week-end as Army was losing to Duke, 6-0. At right, Hall has dismounted while he and Trotter rest. Hall is the son of Mr. and Mrs. John Hall, of 822 Memorial Avenue.

Trotter
1964 Michie Stadium
Jim Hall '65

Trotter (Front) KC Mo (Rear)
1964 Michie Stadium
James Hall '65

Hannibal (L) Pancho (R)
1953 West Point
Bob Chapman '54 (L)
George Perrin '54 (C)
Jan LeCroy '54 (R)

Hannibal
1957
Mule Stable West Point
Don Eckelbarger '53

152

CHAPTER TEN

Conclusion

Mr Jackson (Front) Poncho (Back)
1946 Michie Stadium
Bob Koch '47 (F-Mr Jackson)
Ed Robertson '47 (B-Mr Jackson)
Wally Lukens '47 (on Poncho)

The Long Gray Line is one of America's most respected groups, and the Academy that plays host to these men and women for four years has continued to be a place of mystery, history, and stories passed from generation to generation. The Long Gray Line of mules is much smaller in numbers but filled with stories, pranks, and tradition. The men and women who have grown to know and love these mules over the years all share a profound respect and admiration for the animal that signifies the army.

Eighteen mules have had the honor of being the Official Mascot of the United States. Eighteen mules have impacted the lives of some of the best of the best in America.

I have been honored to care for two of these mules that have served their country dutifully and have thoroughly enjoyed the journey I've taken to learn more about the history of these great animals.

Steve Townes has graciously created an endowment to ensure that the United States Military Academy always has mules.

As of the writing of this book, Stryker, Paladin, and Ranger III are enjoying their time representing West Point and assisting new classes of cadets with pranks that will live on in West Point lore forever.

GO ARMY! BEAT NAVY!

KC MO (Rear) Trotter (Front)
1964 Michie Stadium
James Hall '65 (Front)
Bob Kesmodel '66 (Rear)

Hannibal
1954 West Point Plains
Joseph H. Davis '55

Stryker and Ranger III fitting in right away at Morgan Farms

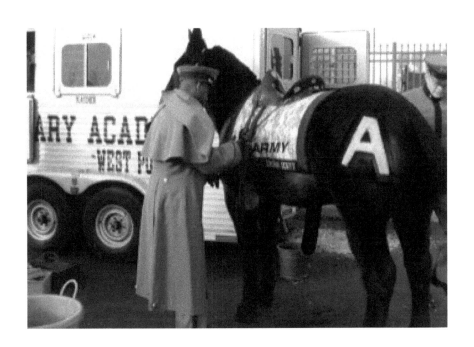

Raider, Ranger II, and General Scott enjoy a summer on Constitution Island.

The fabulous epic of football's greatest "one-two" punch, Felix "Doc" Blanchard and Glenn "Junior" Davis, came to an end on November 30th, 1946, when the rampaging Black Knights of the Hudson and the gallant Middies from the Severn clashed in football's climatic game of the year. And a terrific contest it was too, as the greatly underrated Midshipmen, losers in all but one of their previous contests, refused to admit defeat and kept the issue in doubt right up to the end of the game. The 102,000 fans who crowded every nook and corner of Philadelphia's massive Municipal Stadium gaped in admiration at the inspiring marching of the Cadets and the Middies, laughed with them at the colorful exhibits of pre-game hate put on by both academies, and then settled down to watch two great teams in action. Blanchard and Davis did not disappoint the multitude, for

ARMY 21 . . . NAVY 18

1946

Three of a Kind

Pancho (L) Mr Jackson (R)
1946 Army-Navy Game
Robert Koch '47 (L)
Walter Lukens '47 (Behind)
Ed Robertson '47 (Front)

Pancho (L) Mr Jackson (center)
1946 Location?
Ed Robertson '47 (L)
Robert Koch '47 (center)
W/Friends?

you rather be a mule

KC Mo (L) Trotter (R)
1964 Location?
Bob Kesmodel '66 (L)
James Hall '65 (R)

Hannibal
1948 Location ?
John Jennings '50 (M-2)

"The Army Mule must be restored to the rightful place in our West Point culture. Our mules are symbols of Army toughness, resilience and dignity. Long may they live-and run on the field. Preferably with Mule Riders on them!"

A Message from Tiny Tomsen '54

ABOUT THE AUTHOR

Amanda Van Essen Wirth lives in Hudsonville, MI with her husband, Chris and their children: Noah and Tilly. She is an attorney, JAG Officer, avid traveller and equestrian. She proudly owned Raider who adored her children. She is also one of the many owners of 2020 Kentucky Derby winner, Authentic.

BIBLIOGRAPHY

"A Brief History of West Point." (n.d.) Retrieved from https://www.west-point.edu/about/history-of-west-point.

"A Brief Illustrated History of the Navy Goat." https://news.usni.org/2014/12/12/brief-illustrated-history-navy-goat

"Air Force Falcon" (n.d.) https://www.131bw.ang.af.mil/news/story.asp?id=123353828

Army Field Manuel 3-05.213, Special Forces Use of Pack Animals.

Barnes, Amber, (10/27/2014), https://www.habitatforhorses.org/time-for-a-double-take-a-mules-foal/#:~:text=Mule's%20foal%20fools%20genetics%20with%20%E2%80%9Cimpossible%E2%80%9D%20birth&text=In%20Albania%20in%201994%2C%20it,interest%20from%20the%20scientific%20world.

"Bill the Goat." (n.d.) https://www.usna.edu/PAO/faq_pages/BilltheGoat.php

Bucholtz, Katharina, (08/16/13) "Colorado Miracle Mule Foal Lived Short Life, but Was Well-Loved." Denver Post, https://www.denverpost.com/2013/08/16/colorado-miracle-mule-foal-lived-short-life-but-was-well-loved/

"Cadet Clubs." (04/13/09), https://www.usafa.af.mil/About-Us/Fact-Sheets/Display/Article/428299/cadet-clubs/#:~:text=A%20Peregrine%20falcon%20was%20the,individual%20name%20from%20the%20falconers.

Dotinga, Randy, (06/02/2016), How Smoke the Donkey Made an Unlikely Journey from Iraq to the US, Christian Science Monitor, https://www.csmonitor.com/Books/chapter-and-verse/2016/0602/How-Smoke-the-donkey-made-an-unlikely-journey-from-Iraq-to-the-US

Erlandson, Robert A., "Great Mule Caper detailed, finally Mids nabbed 4 Army Mascots on Eve of Big Game," The Baltimore Sun, (04/28/1992), https://www.baltimoresun.com/news/bs-xpm-1992-04-28-1992119030-story.html

Francis Goes to West Point, (1952), https://www.tcm.com/tcmdb/title/75581/francis-goes-to-west-point#synopsis

Frieberg, John, "Special Forces and Pack Animals-Info and Pubs" The Drive, (06/21/17) https://www.thedrive.com/the-war-zone/11640/u-s-special-operators-are-ready-to-ride-into-war-on-horseback-again

Herodotus, The Histories, 430 B.C.

Lapolla, M., "Our West Point Mules and More..." unpublished.

"Mascot Monday: Blackjack and the Mule" (05/25/09) http://kccollege-gameday.com/2009/05/25/mascot-monday-blackjack-and-the-mule/

Maese, Rick, (11/30/01), "Tired Army Prank Can't Rival Great Navy Heist." The Baltimore Sun https://www.baltimoresun.com/news/bs-xpm-2007-11-30-0711300150-story.html

Martel, Carolyn, (10/08/2015), Donkey's Confused Without Cussing, http://www.mymcr.net/opinion/donkeys-confused-without-cussing/article_9b9b9ea7-3cf8-5d58-9673-8888fc019003.html

"Mule Histories." (n.d.) https://goarmywestpoint.com/sports/2015/3/6/GEN_2014010171.aspx

Nix, Elizabth, "How the Republican and Democratic Parties Got Their Animal Symbols. (08/19/2020), https://www.history.com/news/how-did-the-republican-and-democratic-parties-get-their-animal-symbols

Oettinger, Callie, (12/09/11), "Army Navy:100+ Years in Images" https://www.thehistoryreader.com/military-history/army-navy-football-100-years-images/

Orlean, Susan, "Riding High: Mules in the military," The New Yorker, (02/15/2010) https://www.newyorker.com/magazine/2010/02/15/riding-high

Strasser, Mark, West Point Public Affairs, (12/14/2011)West Point's New Army Mule Mascots Ranger III and Stryker assume duties, https://www.army.mil/article/70764/west_points_new_army_mule_mascots_ranger_iii_stryker_assume_duties

"Ten Famous Omens of the Ancient World." (03/11/14) https://www.ancient-origins.net/myths-legends/ten-famous-and-infamous-omens-ancient-world-001437

Archival Collections

U.S. Department of Defense

United States Military Academy

United States Naval Academy

USMA Mule Museum

Virginia Military Academy

Special Thanks For Personal Interviews, Conversations, Photographs, and Papers

Doug Doan

Ambassador Al Hoffman

Michael Lapolla

Harrison Mann

David Nunneley

Walter Price

Tiny Tomsen

Steve Townes

Betty Williams

-All of you Army officers and mule enthusiasts that have had conversations with me over the years

Most of the information in this book came from the incredible scrapbooks and information I was gifted from the men that most loved the mules!

PHOTO INDEX

The appearance of U.S. Department of Defense visual information does not imply or constitute DoD endorsement.

The appearance of U.S. Army. U.S. Air Force, U.S. Navy visual information or sources does not imply or constitute endorsement.

This is not an official publication of or written in collaboration with the United States Military Academy.

Page 5 PDF: Photo from U.S. Army

Page 7 PDF: Photo from U.S. Army

Page 9 PDF: Photo from U.S. Army

Page 11 PDF: Photo by Amanda V. Wirth

Page 2: Photo by Amanda V. Wirth

Page 4: Photo of Tiny Tomsen's scrapbooks provided by Mike Lapolla

Page 6: Photo from U.S. Army

Page 7: Photo from U.S. Army

Page 8: Photo from Mike Lapolla

Page 9: Photo of Tiny Tomsen's scrapbooks provided by Mike Lapolla

Page 10: Photos from Christopher Wirth

Page 13: Photo of the Cover of the West Point Discovery Children's Book from Tiny Tomsen

Page 14: Photo from U.S. Army

Page 16: Photo by Amanda V. Wirth

Page 17: Photo from Mike Lapolla

Page 18: Both photos from U.S. Army

Page 19: Photo from U.S. Army, 2007

Page 20: Photo still from U.S. Army video

Page 21: Photo still from U.S. Army video

Page 22: "Babe Ruth and Attendants with Army Mule." Photographer: Bettman. Licensed from Getty Images

Page 23: Photo from Harrison Mann

Page 24: Photo signed to Mr. Hendricks and given to Tiny Tomsen. Provided by Mike Lapolla

Page 25: Photo of Tiny Tomsen's scrapbooks provided by Mike Lapolla

Page 27: Signed Photo of 1936 Army/Washington Lee Football Program from Tiny Tomsen and Mike Lapolla

Page 28: U.S. Army

Page 29: U.S. Army

Page 30: Both photos: Photo of Tiny Tomsen's scrapbooks provided by Mike Lapolla

Page 31: Photo of Tiny Tomsen's scrapbooks provided by Mike Lapolla

Page 33: Photo of Tiny Tomsen's scrapbooks provided by Mike Lapolla

Page 34: U.S. Army

Page 35: U.S. Army

Page 36: Mike Lapolla's photo of the Trotter description at the Mule Museum

Page 37: Photos from Tiny Tomsen of "Trotter Goes to West Point from Western Horseman, January 1958

Page 38: Photos from Tiny Tomsen of "Trotter Goes to West Point from Western Horseman, January 1958

Page 38: Bottom photos from Tiny Tomsen's collection originally from U.S. Army Signal Corps.

Page 40: Both photos: U.S. Army

Page 41:U.S. Army

Page 42: Photo of Tiny Tomsen's scrapbooks provided by Mike Lapolla

Page 43: U.S. Army

Page 44: U.S. Army

Page 45: Photos of scrapbook items from Tiny Tomsen

Page 46: Top photo from U.S. Army, Photos from Tiny Tomsen and his photo of the cover of Rural Arkansas.

Page 47: Tiny Tomsen's Photos of the Rural Arkansas Article

Page 48: Tiny Tomsen's Photo of the Rural Arkansas Article

Page 49: U.S. Army, 2011

Page 50, Top Photo: Harrison Mann, Bottom Photo: U.S. Army

Page 52: Photo from 2008 article of the Pointer View by Emily Tower.

Page 53: Both photos, U.S. Army, 2011

Page 55: U.S. Army, 2011

Page 56: U.S. Army, 2011

Page 57: U.S. Army, 2011

Page 58: Top: U.S. Army Signal Corps., 1122/1953. Signal Corps Number: 53-30-145-1197

Page 59: U.S. Army

Page 61: Still from U.S. Army video

Page 62: U.S. Army, 2011

Page 63: Photo provided by Mike Lapolla

Page 64: Top: U.S. Department of Defense, December 7, 2012, Photo ID: 780941-I-UUS90-189.jpg
Bottom: U.S. Department of Defense, December 12, 2014, Photo ID: 696646-X-RGR77-183.jpg

Page 65: Photo of Tiny Tomsen's scrapbooks provided by Mike Lapolla

Page 66: Photo of Tiny Tomsen's scrapbooks provided by Mike Lapolla

Page 68: Photos provided by Mike Lapolla

Page 69: U.S. Army Signal Corps. 11/22/1953. Signal Corp Number: 53-30-145-1193

Page 71: U.S. Army

Page 72: Photo of Tiny Tomsen's scrapbooks provided by Mike Lapolla

Page 73: Photo of Tiny Tomsen's scrapbooks provided by Mike Lapolla

Page 75: U.S. Army Photographer Kepler. US Army Signal Corps. Signal Corps Number: (30-145)31/ Ah-54. 11/28/1954

Page 76: Photo of Tiny Tomsen's scrapbooks provided by Mike Lapolla

Page 77: Photo from Steve Townes

Page 78: Photo from Harrison Mann

Page 81: Photos from Mike Lapolla and Tiny Tomsen

Page 82: Photos from Mike Lapolla and Tiny Tomsen

Page 83: U.S. Navy, Photo ID: 101211-F-668S-161

Page 85: Photos from Mike Lapolla Book

Page 87: Top Photo: Photographer Wroughton. United States Army, Signal Corps. 11/22/1953 Signal Corps Number: (30-145)1203/Ah-53; Bottom Photo: photo from Mike Lapolla's book.

Page 88: Photos from Mike Lapolla's Book

Page 93: Photo of Tiny Tomsen's scrapbooks provided by Mike Lapolla

Page 94: Photo from Mike Lapolla and Tiny Tomsen

Page 96: All Photos from United States Naval Academy Public Affairs Office

Page 99: Photos provided by Mike Lapolla

Page 100: Rivalry description Photo provided by Mike Lapolla, Goat photo from United States Naval Academy Public Affairs Office.

Page 101: U.S. Army

Page 102: Photo from Harrison Mann

Page 103: U.S. Army, 2011

Page 105: Photo from Mike Lapolla

Page 106: Photos from Mike Lapolla and Harrison Mann

Page 107: Photo from Harrison Mann

Page 108: Army Field Manual 3-05.213, Special Forces Use of Pack Animals, Figure 6-5

Page 109: Top: Army Field Manual 3-05.213, Special Forces Use of Pack Animals, Figure 5-1, Bottom: Army Field Manual 3-05.213, Special Forces Use of Pack Animals, Figure 5-2

Page 110: Army Field Manual 3-05.213, Special Forces Use of Pack Animals, Figure 5-3, and Army Field Manual 3-05.213, Special Forces Use of Pack Animals, Figure 5-4

Page 111: Army Field Manual 3-05.213, Special Forces Use of Pack Animals, Figure 6-1

Page 112: Army Field Manual 3-05.213, Special Forces Use of Pack Animals, Figure 6-3

Page 113: Photos from Mike Lapolla

Page 114: Photo from Mike Lapolla

Page 115: Photos from Mike Lapolla

Page 116: Photos from Mike Lapolla

Page 117: Photos from Mike Lapolla

Page 118: Photo from Mike Lapolla

Page 119: Photos from Mike Lapolla

Page 120: Photos from Mike Lapolla

Page 121: Photo from Mike Lapolla

Page 122: Photos from Mike Lapolla

Page 123: Photos from Mike Lapolla

Page 124: Photo from Mike Lapolla

Page 126: Photo from Mike Lapolla

Page 127: Photo provided my Mike Lapolla. Photo of the "Kicking A Statuette" originally commissioned by Tiny Tomsen.

Page 129: Photo from Mike Lapolla

Page 130: J. David Nunneley

Page 132: J. David Nunneley

Page 133: J. David Nunneley, Mike Lapolla, and Tiny Tomsen

Page 134: Drawing from J. David Nunneley and photo of program from Mike Lapolla

Page 135: Photos from Mike Lapolla

Page 136: Photos Mike Lapolla, Tiny Tomsen, and Steve Townes

Page 137: Photos from Mike Lapolla, Tiny Tomsen, and Steve Townes

Page 138: Photos Mike Lapolla, Tiny Tomsen, and Steve Townes

Page 139: Photo from Mike Lapolla

Page 140: Photos Mike Lapolla, Tiny Tomsen, and Steve Townes

Page 141: Photos Mike Lapolla, Tiny Tomsen, and Steve Townes

Page 142: Photo from U.S. Army

Page 143: Photos by Amanda V. Wirth

Page 144: Photo by Amanda V. Wirth

Page 148: Photo of Tiny Tomsen's scrapbooks provided by Mike Lapolla

Page 149: Autographed poster provided by Tiny Tomsen and Mike Lapolla

Page 150: Photo of Tiny Tomsen's scrapbooks provided by Mike Lapolla

Page 151: Photo of Tiny Tomsen's scrapbooks provided by Mike Lapolla

Page 152: Photo of Tiny Tomsen's scrapbooks provided by Mike Lapolla

Page 153: Photo of Tiny Tomsen's scrapbooks provided by Mike Lapolla

Page 154: Photo of Tiny Tomsen's scrapbooks provided by Mike Lapolla

Page 155: Photo of Tiny Tomsen's scrapbooks provided by Mike Lapolla

Page 156: Photos from Mike Lapolla and photoshopped photos circulated by Steve Townes.

Page 157: Photos from Harrison Mann

Page 158: Photos from Harrison Mann

Page 159: Photo of Tiny Tomsen's scrapbooks provided by Mike Lapolla

Page 160: Photo of Tiny Tomsen's scrapbooks provided by Mike Lapolla

Page 161: Photo of Tiny Tomsen's scrapbooks provided by Mike Lapolla

Page 162: Photo of Tiny Tomsen's scrapbooks provided by Mike Lapolla

Page 163: Photo of Tiny Tomsen's scrapbooks provided by Mike Lapolla

Page 164: Photo by Christopher Wirth

ENDNOTES

1   "A Brief History of West Point." (n.d.) Retrieved from https://www.westpoint.edu/about/history-of-west-point

2   Army Field Manuel 3-05.213, Special Forces Use of Pack Animals Section 2.1

3   Army Field Manuel 3-05.213, Special Forces Use of Pack Animals Section 2.2

4   Army Field Manuel 3-05.213, Special Forces Use of Pack Animals Section 2.3

5   Stories About Using Mules in Burma. (05/16/19) Retrieved from https://www.fold3.com/page/642792606/using-mules-in-burma

5b   Orlean, Susan, "Riding High: Mules in the military," The New Yorker, (02/15/2010) https://www.newyorker.com/magazine/2010/02/15/riding-high

6   Frieberg, John, "Special Forces and Pack Animals-Info and Pubs" (06/21/17) https://www.thedrive.com/the-war-zone/11640/u-s-special-operators-are-ready-to-ride-into-war-on-horseback-again

7   Lapolla, M., "Our West Point Mules and More..." unpublished.

8   "Mule Histories." (n.d.) https://goarmywestpoint.com/sports/2015/3/6/GEN_2014010171.aspx

9   "Mule Histories." (n.d.) https://goarmywestpoint.com/sports/2015/3/6/GEN_2014010171.aspx

10   "Mule Histories." (n.d.) https://goarmywestpoint.com/sports/2015/3/6/GEN_2014010171.aspx

11   "Mule Histories." (n.d.) https://goarmywestpoint.com/sports/2015/3/6/GEN_2014010171.aspx

12   "Mule Histories." (n.d.) https://goarmywestpoint.com/sports/2015/3/6/GEN_2014010171.aspx

13   "Mule Histories." (n.d.) https://goarmywestpoint.com/sports/2015/3/6/GEN_2014010171.aspx

14   "Mule Histories." (n.d.) https://goarmywestpoint.com/sports/2015/3/6/GEN_2014010171.aspx

15   "Mule Histories." (n.d.) https://goarmywestpoint.com/sports/2015/3/6/GEN_2014010171.aspx

16   "Mule Histories." (n.d.) https://goarmywestpoint.com/sports/2015/3/6/GEN_2014010171.aspx

17   "Mule Histories." (n.d.) https://goarmywestpoint.com/sports/2015/3/6/GEN_2014010171.aspx

18   "Mule Histories." (n.d.) https://goarmywestpoint.com/sports/2015/3/6/GEN_2014010171.aspx

19   "Mule Histories." (n.d.) https://goarmywestpoint.com/sports/2015/3/6/GEN_2014010171.aspx

20   "Mule Histories." (n.d.) https://goarmywestpoint.com/sports/2015/3/6/GEN_2014010171.aspx

21   Interview with Betty Williams

22   Page 56-59, Strasser, Mark, West Point Public Affairs, (12/14/2011)" West Point's New Army Mule Mascots Ranger III and Stryker assume duties," https://www.army.mil/article/70764/west_points_new_army_mule_mascots_ranger_iii_stryker_assume_duties

23   Email from Steve Townes (12/03/2011) The Mule Change of Command 2011

24   Mule Rider list compiled by Tiny Tomsen

25   Email from Walter Price. (01/29/2012)

26   Phone conversations with Al Hoffman, 2012

27   Phone conversations with Al Hoffman, 2012

28   Phone conversations with Steve Townes, 2012

29   Phone conversations with Steve Townes, 2012.

30   Photo and Caption released by the U.S. Navy with ID 101211-F-668S-161

31   Erlandson, Robert A., "Great Mule Caper detailed, finally Mids nabbed 4 Army Mascots on Eve of Big Game," The Baltimore Sun (04/28/1992), https://www.baltimoresun.com/news/bs-xpm-1992-04-28-1992119030-story.html

32   provided by Lapolla, M. Abstracted from Ben Schemmer's eulogy.

33   Phone conversation with Steve Townes, 2012.

34   Phone conversation with Steve Townes, 2012.

35   Bucholtz, Katharina, (08/16/13) "Colorado Miracle Mule Foal Lived Short Life, but Was Well-Loved." The Denver Post, https://www.denverpost.com/2013/08/16/colorado-miracle-mule-foal-lived-short-life-but-was-well-loved/

36   Barnes, Amber, (10/27/2014), https://www.habitatforhorses.org/time-for-a-double-take-a-mules-foal/#:~:text=Mule's%20foal%20fools%20genetics%20with%20%E2%80%9Cimpossible%E2%80%9D%20birth&text=In%20Albania%20in%201994%2C%20it,interest%20from%20the%20scientific%20world.

37   Herodotus, The Histories, 430 B.C.

38   "Bill the Goat." (n.d.)

39   "Cadet Clubs." (04/13/09), https://www.usafa.af.mil/About-Us/Fact-Sheets/Display/Article/428299/cadet-clubs/#:~:text=A%20Peregrine%20falcon%20was%20the,individual%20name%20from%20the%20falconers.

40   SFC Robert P. Johnson plaque within the Mule Museum and outside the Mule Museum.

41   written By M. Lapolla (2020)

42   Lapolla, M. "Our West Point Mules and More..."

43   Nunnelly, D. Phone Interview, 2020

44   Martel, Carolyn, (10/08/2015), Donkey's Confused Without Cussing, http://www.mymcr.net/opinion/donkeys-confused-without-cussing/article_9b9b9ea7-3cf8-5d58-9673-8888fc019003.html

45   Dotinga, Randy, (06/02/2016), "How Smoke the Donkey Made an Unlikely Journey from Iraq to the US," Christian Science Monitor, https://www.csmonitor.com/Books/chapter-and-verse/2016/0602/How-Smoke-the-donkey-made-an-unlikely-journey-from-Iraq-to-the-US

46   Francis Goes to West Point, (1952), https://www.tcm.com/tcmdb/title/75581/francis-goes-to-west-point#synopsis

47   Nix, Elizabth, "How the Republican and Democratic Parties Got Their Animal Symbols. (08/19/2020), https://www.history.com/news/how-did-the-republican-and-democratic-parties-get-their-animal-symbols